DO YOU KNOW...

What a sommelier is...?
Who painted *La Primavera*...?
What the Queen's second name is...?
What did the ancient Greeks and Romans use
a strigil for...?
Where the wettest place in the world is...?

The answers to these and hundreds of other brain-teasing
questions are in this book, designed to give you hours of
fun and challenge as you pit your wits in one of the most
original and exciting quiz books ever. Whether you're a
lazybones or a mastermind, this is the book for you!

# *The New Pears Family Quiz Book*

**GYLES BRANDRETH**

**WARNER BOOKS**

A *Warner* Book

First published in Great Britain by Sphere Books Ltd 1989
Reprinted by Warner Books 1993
Reprinted 1994

Typeset by Leaper & Gard Ltd, Bristol, England
Printed in England by Clays Ltd, St Ives plc

ISBN 0 7515 08632

Warner Books
A Division of
Little, Brown and Company (UK)
Brettenham House
Lancaster Place
London WC2E 7EN

# CONTENTS

# INTRODUCTION

Intended as fun for all members of the family, this book contains 100 quizzes, half of which are on specific subjects, and half which are a real hotch potch of topics, which is why they are called 'A Mixed Bag'.

Each quiz has ten questions, and each question has four alternative answers. The idea is to try to answer the questions without looking at the alternatives, but to use them if you get stuck.

To use this book as a family, get one person to act as quizmaster. He or she should read out the questions one at a time, without giving the alternative answers, and award two points to the person who answers a question correctly. If no one can answer a particular question, the quizmaster can read out the alternative answers, and then award one point to the person who picks the correct answer.

If you are reading the book alone, cover up the alternative answers and award yourself two points for each answer you get right, and one point for each answered correctly if you have to use the alternative answers.

If you are still stuck, then the correct answers are given at the back of the book.

These suggested methods should be used wherever possible.

I hope *The New Pears Family Quiz Book* will provide you with hours of pleasant, head-scratching amusement.

GYLES BRANDRETH

# 100 QUIZZES

# A MIXED BAG

1. **Who owns the Castle of Mey?**
   Is it:
   - a. The Queen?
   - b. The Queen Mother?
   - c. The Duke of Argyll?
   - d. The National Trust?

2. **When is Lammas?**
   Is it:
   - a. 1 May?
   - b. 1 August?
   - c. 1 September?
   - d. 1 October?

3. **Which was the first airport to have its own railway station?**
   Was it:
   - a. Gatwick?
   - b. Heathrow?
   - c. Orly?
   - d. Kennedy?

4. **Who wrote *The Thin Man*?**
   Was it:
   - a. F. Scott Fitzgerald?
   - b. Raymond Chandler?
   - c. Ian Fleming?
   - d. Dashiel Hammett?

5. **Who was Alvar Aalto?**
   Was he:
   - a. A pop singer?
   - b. Secretary-General of the United Nations?
   - c. An architect?
   - d. A Booker Prize winner?

6. **Which is the largest lake in the Lake District?**
   Is it:
       a. Ullswater?
       b. Windermere?
       c. Derwentwater?
       d. Coniston Water?

7. **Silvanus was the Roman god of what?**
   Was it:
       a. Hunting?
       b. Vineyards?
       c. Male sexuality?
       d. Trees and forests?

8. **Who or what is Ben Macdhui?**
   Is it:
       a. The UK's second highest mountain?
       b. A Scottish poet?
       c. An island in the Outer Hebrides?
       d. A malt whisky?

9. **In which city might you see a Broadway show?**
       a. Chicago?
       b. Los Angeles?
       c. San Francisco?
       d. New York?

10. **What connects Bognor, Kingsbury, Milton and Rowley?**
   Is it:
       a. All have a Lord Mayor?
       b. The Queen has homes in all of them?
       c. All have Roman remains?
       d. All have the suffix 'Regis'?

# HOME, SWEET HOME

1.  **What, in building terms, do the initials DPC stand for?**
    **Is it:**
    a.  Drainpipe cutter?
    b.  Damp-proof course?
    c.  Damp protection coupling?
    d.  Drawn-pug construction?

2.  **What is a lintel?**
    **Is it:**
    a.  A horizontal bar over a doorway or window frame?
    b.  One of two vertical uprights either side of a door or window frame?
    c.  A horizontal timber or stone at the bottom of a door or window frame?
    d.  A kind of vegetable?

3.  **What is pargetting?**
    **Is it:**
    a.  Roofing with wooden tiles?
    b.  Roofing with clay tiles?
    c.  Mortar between bricks which has been raked out or recessed?
    d.  Outdoor plaster with an ornamental pattern?

4.  **What is a string course?**
    **Is it:**
    a.  A course of brickwork containing slate to prevent rising damp?
    b.  A course of brickwork which projects beyond the others?
    c.  The course of brickwork beneath a window?
    d.  The course of brickwork at the top of a wall where it meets the roof?

5. **What is ashlar?**
   Is it:
   - a. Square-cut stone?
   - b. Roofing felt?
   - c. Rubble into which paving stones are set?
   - d. The lining of drainage channels?

6. **What is a baluster?**
   Is it:
   - a. A brass door knob?
   - b. A handrail?
   - c. The parapet of a terrace or balcony?
   - d. One of a row of short pillars?

7. **What is a transom?**
   Is it:
   - a. A ditch dug to accommodate a building's foundations?
   - b. A bricklayer's trowel?
   - c. The pulley around which the rope of a sash window runs?
   - d. The horizontal bar of a window?

8. **What is a mullion?**
   Is it:
   - a. The vertical bar between the panes of a window?
   - b. One of the vertical sides of a fireplace?
   - c. A fungicide paint applied under plaster?
   - d. An old iron cooking range?

9. **What shape is a gothic arch?**
   Is it:
   - a. Square at the top?
   - b. Pointed at the top?
   - c. Rounded at the top?
   - d. Having a double curve at the top?

10. **What is a corbel?**
    Is it:
    - a. A unit used for measuring sand and cement?
    - b. An ornamental collar surrounding a chimney?
    - c. A clamp for fixing scaffolding poles together?
    - d. A projection of timber or stone jutting out from a wall?

# A MIXED BAG

1.  **How deep is a fathom?**
    Is it:
    - a. 3 feet?
    - b. 5 feet?
    - c. 6 feet?
    - d. 12 feet?

2.  **What is a cavy?**
    Is it:
    - a. A pot-holer?
    - b. A guinea pig?
    - c. A miner's helmet?
    - d. A type of belt?

3.  **What is Dennis the Menace's dog called?**
    Is it:
    - a. Rover?
    - b. Samson?
    - c. Jaws?
    - d. Gnasher?

4.  **What is Jodrell Bank?**
    Is it:
    - a. An observatory in Cheshire?
    - b. An area of the North Sea?
    - c. The financial centre of the Isle of Man?
    - d. A fence in the Hickstead show-jumping course?

5.  **Whose arch enemy was Professor Moriarty?**
    Was he the enemy of:
    - a. Sherlock Holmes?
    - b. James Bond?
    - c. Richard Hannay?
    - d. Biggles?

6. **Where is Rotten Row?**
   Is it:
   - a. In Sussex?
   - b. In London's Hyde Park?
   - c. In Paris?
   - d. In Shanghai?

7. **What is the boiling point of water?**
   Is it:
   - a. $100°F$?
   - b. $212°F$?
   - c. $212°C$?
   - d. $98.4°F$?

8. **What was Paddington Bear's favourite food?**
   Was it:
   - a. Honey?
   - b. Jam?
   - c. Marmalade?
   - d. Chocolate?

9. **What have Evian, Malvern and San Pellegrino in common?**
   Is it that:
   - a. All have music festivals in July?
   - b. All have famous Roman remains?
   - c. All are situated more than 1000 feet above sea level?
   - d. All are sources of spring water?

10. **What was Ronald Reagan *before* he was an actor?**
    Was he:
    - a. A professional boxer?
    - b. A sports commentator?
    - c. A journalist?
    - d. A shoe salesman?

# WINING AND DINING

1. **What fish does caviare come from?**
   Is it:
   - a. Sole?
   - b. Salmon?
   - c. Sturgeon?
   - d. Trout?

2. **Which of the following is a famous French dessert wine?**
   Is it:
   - a. Romanée-Conti?
   - b. Château Talbot?
   - c. Château Mouton Rothschild?
   - d. Château d'Yquem?

3. **Dorset Blue Vinny, Cornish Yarg, Teifi and Belstone are all types of what?**
   Are they:
   - a. Sheep?
   - b. Cheeses?
   - c. Ciders?
   - d. Wines?

4. **What is a sommelier?**
   Is it:
   - a. A wine waiter?
   - b. A wine cooler?
   - c. A covered dish for keeping food warm?
   - d. A sauce served with salmon?

5. **If you were eating Crêpes Suzette, would you have:**
   - a. Wild mushrooms cooked with garlic and wine?
   - b. Strawberry meringue and cream?
   - c. Pancakes cooked with brandy and liqueur?
   - d. Pancakes filled with apple slices and served with cream?

6. **What is a 'horse's neck'?**
   Is it:
   - a. A dessert made from a curved sponge cake, set with fruit?
   - b. A biscuit served with port?
   - c. A drink made from chilled white wine and soda?
   - d. A cocktail made from brandy and dry ginger, served with a piece of orange peel?

7. **What is a marinade?**
   Is it:
   - a. A mixture of wine, oil, herbs and vegetables in which meat is soaked?
   - b. A sauce made of wine, herbs and vegetables?
   - c. A mixture of roughly diced vegetables, cooked in olive oil?
   - d. A pan in which fish is cooked?

8. **Which of the following cheeses is made from ewes' milk?**
   Is it:
   - a. Brie?
   - b. Camembert?
   - c. Bresse Bleu?
   - d. Roquefort?

9. **What is bouillabaisse?**
   Is it:
   - a. A soup made with onions and cheese?
   - b. A Provençal fish stew?
   - c. A mousse made with smoked salmon and caviare?
   - d. A sauce served with steak, made from brandy, cream and peppercorns?

10. **What kind of wine is made from these vine stocks: Chardonnay, Pinot Noir and Pinot Meunier?**
    Is it:
    - a. White burgundy?
    - b. Claret?
    - c. Hock?
    - d. Champagne?

# A MIXED BAG

1. **What is a hoodoo?**
   Is it:
   - a. A strangely shaped column of rock?
   - b. A voodoo ceremony?
   - c. Something that brings good luck?
   - d. A cave formed by sea action?

2. **Why was Walter Crane famous?**
   Was it as:
   - a. A poet and author of *The Bridge*?
   - b. The inventor of the lawn mower?
   - c. The discoverer of the vaccine for typhoid?
   - d. An illustrator of children's books?

3. **Where is Belleek pottery made?**
   Is it in:
   - a. England?
   - b. Ireland?
   - c. Scotland?
   - d. Wales?

4. **In which city is the area of SoHo located?**
   Is it in:
   - a. Paris?
   - b. London?
   - c. New York?
   - d. Rome?

5. **What is a hyperplane?**
   Is it:
   - a. A seaplane?
   - b. A mathematical term?
   - c. A sailing term?
   - d. A high level of activity?

6. **In which English village did Canute command the tide to roll back?**
   Was it:
   - a. Rye?
   - b. West Wittering?
   - c. West Lulworth?
   - d. Bosham?

7. **What is a barquentine?**
   Is it:
   - a. A cocktail?
   - b. Bark from an Amazonian tree?
   - c. A ship?
   - d. Quarantine of a ship?

8. **Where does the spice saffron come from?**
   Is it:
   - a. The flowers of the daffodil?
   - b. The leaves of the ash tree?
   - c. The bulbs of narcissus?
   - d. The stigmas of crocus?

9. **What is a gnomon?**
   Is it:
   - a. A rod which shows the time?
   - b. A thought or a judgement?
   - c. A goblin?
   - d. An elf-like garden figure?

10. **Who founded Eton College?**
    Was it:
    - a. Henry VIII?
    - b. Henry VI?
    - c. Cardinal Wolsey?
    - d. Edward VII?

# THE SPORT OF KINGS

1.  **Which organisation controls flat racing and steeplechasing in Great Britain?**
    Is it:
    - a. The British Horse Society?
    - b. The National Hunt Committee?
    - c. Tattersall's?
    - d. The Jockey Club?

2.  **How long is the Grand National course?**
    Is it:
    - a. Just over 3 miles (5 kilometres)?
    - b. Just over 4 miles (6 kilometres)?
    - c. Just over 5 miles (8 kilometres)?
    - d. Just over 6 miles (10 kilometres)?

3.  **How many days does Royal Ascot last?**
    Is it:
    - a. Two days?
    - b. Three days?
    - c. Four days?
    - d. Five days?

4.  **Where is the St Leger run?**
    Is it:
    - a. Aintree?
    - b. Ascot?
    - c. Doncaster?
    - d. Epsom?

5.  **What is significant about the 1000 Guineas, the Oaks and the Coronation Stakes?**
    Is it:
    - a. They are all run in June?
    - b. They are all run at Epsom?
    - c. They are all races for fillies only?
    - d. They are all races for colts only?

6. **Who won the Derby in 1988?**
   **Was it:**
   - a. Ravinella?
   - b. Kahyasi?
   - c. Shahrastani?
   - d. Unfuwain?

7. **Which three races constitute the British Triple Crown?**
   **Are they:**
   - a. The 2000 Guineas, the Derby and the St Leger?
   - b. The Derby, the Ascot Gold Cup, the Oaks?
   - c. The Grand National, the Cheltenham Gold Cup, the Cesarewitch?
   - d. The Royal Hunt Cup, the Ebor Handicap, the Lincoln Handicap?

8. **Who or what is Luca Cumani?**
   **Is he:**
   - a. A horse?
   - b. A jockey?
   - c. A trainer?
   - d. An owner?

9. **Why is Red Rum famous?**
   **Is it because:**
   - a. He won the Grand National in three consecutive years?
   - b. He won the Derby in three consecutive years?
   - c. He won the Grand National three times?
   - d. He won the Grand National four times?

10. **Where is the Prix de L'Arc de Triomphe run?**
    **Is it at:**
    - a. Longchamp?
    - b. Deauville?
    - c. Chantilly?
    - d. Auteuil?

# A MIXED BAG

1.  **Where is the Aral Sea?**
    Is it:
    - a. In Antarctica?
    - b. In the USSR?
    - c. Off the north coast of Norway?
    - d. Between the USSR and Alaska?

2.  **Who wrote *La Morte D'Arthur*?**
    Was it:
    - a. George Bernard Shaw?
    - b. Geoffrey Chaucer?
    - c. Sir Walter Scott?
    - d. Sir Thomas Malory?

3.  **When does the Royal Maundy ceremony take place?**
    Is it:
    - a. 15 February?
    - b. Boxing Day?
    - c. The Thursday before Good Friday?
    - d. The Thursday after Easter?

4.  **Who painted *Guernica*?**
    Was it:
    - a. Salvador Dali?
    - b. Picasso?
    - c. Goya?
    - d. Velasquez?

5.  **How was/is Lady Mallowan better known?**
    Was/is it as:
    - a. The ballerina Alicia Markova?
    - b. The spy Mata Hari?
    - c. The actress Peggy Ashcroft?
    - d. The writer Agatha Christie?

6. **What was the name of the ferryman who carried the souls of the dead across the River Styx?**
Was it:
   - a. Charon?
   - b. Cerberus?
   - c. Pluto?
   - d. Ceres?

7. **Who is Duke of Rothesay, Earl of Carrick, Baron Renfrew, Lord of the Isles and Great Steward of Scotland?**
Is it:
   - a. The Duke of Edinburgh?
   - b. Prince Charles?
   - c. Prince Andrew?
   - d. The Duke of Atholl?

8. **In which British city is the Crucible Theatre?**
Is it in:
   - a. Birmingham?
   - b. Bristol?
   - c. Sheffield?
   - d. Hull?

9. **Where is the biggest bell in the world?**
Is it:
   - a. In St Paul's Cathedral?
   - b. In the Kremlin?
   - c. In Durham Cathedral?
   - d. In Notre-Dame, Paris?

10. **Winston Churchill and Harold Wilson had at least one thing in common. What was it?**
Was it:
   - a. Their height?
   - b. Their university college?
   - c. Their school?
   - d. The names of their children?

# ALL THE WORLD'S A STAGE

1. **Which theatre company performs in the Olivier, Lyttelton and Cottesloe Theatres?**
   Is it:
   - a. The Royal Shakespeare Company?
   - b. Shared Experience?
   - c. The National Theatre?
   - d. The Renaissance Theatre Company?

2. **Who was the first actor to receive a knighthood?**
   Was it:
   - a. Laurence Olivier?
   - b. John Gielgud?
   - c. Henry Irving?
   - d. Edmund Kean?

3. **Andrew Lloyd Webber wrote the music for three of these shows. Which is the odd one out?**
   Is it:
   - a. *Starlight Express*?
   - b. *Chess*?
   - c. *Cats*?
   - d. *Evita*?

4. **Which theatre was famous for its farces?**
   Was it:
   - a. The Savoy?
   - b. The Comedy?
   - c. The Playhouse?
   - d. The Whitehall?

5. **Which theatre is the home of the English National Opera?**
   Is it:
   - a. Sadler's Wells?
   - b. The Garrick?
   - c. The Royal Opera House?
   - d. The Coliseum?

6. **In which city is the Citizens' Theatre?**
   Is it in:
   - a. Edinburgh?
   - b. Glasgow?
   - c. Manchester?
   - d. Aberdeen?

7. **Who wrote the book on which the stage musical *Les Misérables* is based?**
   Was it:
   - a. Victor Hugo?
   - b. Molière?
   - c. Emile Zola?
   - d. Gustave Flaubert?

8. **Which show holds the record for the world's longest run?**
   Is it:
   - a. *Run for Your Wife!*?
   - b. *No Sex, Please, We're British*?
   - c. *Nicholas Nickelby*?
   - d. *The Mousetrap*?

9. **In which of London's parks is there an open-air theatre?**
   Is it in:
   - a. Hyde Park?
   - b. Regent's Park?
   - c. Kensington Gardens?
   - d. St James's Park?

10. **To what did His Majesty's Theatre change its name in 1952?**
    Was it to:
    - a. Her Majesty's Theatre?
    - b. The Duke of York's Theatre?
    - c. The Queen's Theatre?
    - d. The Duchess Theatre?

# A MIXED BAG

1. **What is Chantilly?**
   **Is it:**
   - a. A sweet sparkling wine?
   - b. A type of brandy?
   - c. A type of truffle?
   - d. A type of lace?

2. **What does the Roman numeral L stand for?**
   **Is it:**
   - a. 40?
   - b. 50?
   - c. 500?
   - d. 1000?

3. **Whose ship was the *Golden Hind*?**
   **Did it belong to:**
   - a. Sir Walter Raleigh?
   - b. Sir Francis Drake?
   - c. Lord Nelson?
   - d. Christopher Columbus?

4. **What is the 'Ham and High'?**
   **Is it:**
   - a. A cut of bacon?
   - b. A famous London pub?
   - c. A North London newspaper?
   - d. A traditional Wiltshire festival?

5. **Who came from the doomed planet Krypton?**
   **Was it:**
   - a. Dr Who?
   - b. The Daleks?
   - c. Superman?
   - d. Mr Spock?

6. **What does the word *queue* mean in French?**
   Is it:
   - a. Queue?
   - b. To stand?
   - c. To wait?
   - d. Tail?

7. **What is a wether?**
   Is it:
   - a. A shellfish?
   - b. An aimless conflict?
   - c. A castrated male sheep?
   - d. A bad spell of weather?

8. **Who is the patron saint of travellers?**
   Is it:
   - a. St Francis?
   - b. St Christopher?
   - c. St Jude?
   - d. St Thomas?

9. **How many counters does each player have in draughts?**
   Is it:
   - a. Four?
   - b. Eight?
   - c. Twelve?
   - d. Twenty?

10. **What is a sulky?**
    Is it:
    - a. A bad-tempered child?
    - b. A carriage used in harness racing in the USA?
    - c. A bobbin used in silk spinning?
    - d. A mythical sea creature, half seal, half man?

# TOURISTS' EUROPE

1.  **In which European city is the Rijksmuseum?**
    Is it in:
    - a.  Antwerp?
    - b.  Brussels?
    - c.  Bruges?
    - d.  Amsterdam?

2.  **In which Italian city does the race called the Palio take place?**
    Is it in:
    - a.  Padua?
    - b.  Siena?
    - c.  Naples?
    - d.  Milan?

3.  **Where is Lac Leman?**
    Is it near:
    - a.  Geneva?
    - b.  Annecy?
    - c.  Grenoble?
    - d.  Marseille?

4.  **Which of these Greek islands is *not* in the Cyclades?**
    Is it:
    - a.  Paros?
    - b.  Ios?
    - c.  Rhodes?
    - d.  Naxos?

5.  **In which European city could you see a display by the Spanish Riding School?**
    Would it be in:
    - a.  Madrid?
    - b.  Barcelona?
    - c.  Vienna?
    - d.  Paris?

6. **In which part of France is Anjou?**
   Is it in:
   - a. The north?
   - b. The south?
   - c. The east?
   - d. The west?

7. **Which Italian city is known as *La Serenissima*?**
   Is it:
   - a. Venice?
   - b. Rome?
   - c. Florence?
   - d. Genoa?

8. **Where is the Alhambra Palace?**
   Is it in:
   - a. Madrid?
   - b. Bilbao?
   - c. Cordoba?
   - d. Granada?

9. **A town called Brig is at the end of one Alpine tunnel. Which one?**
   Is it the:
   - a. Mont Blanc?
   - b. Simplon?
   - c. St Gotthard?
   - d. St Bernard?

10. **In which city is the famous statue called the *Manneken-pis*?**
    Is it in:
    - a. Brussels?
    - b. Copenhagen?
    - c. Paris?
    - d. The Hague?

# A MIXED BAG

1. **Who was the first English monarch to be formally styled with a post-nominal number?**
   Was it:
   - a. Elizabeth I?
   - b. Henry VIII?
   - c. William II?
   - d. George I?

2. **What is the IMF?**
   Is it:
   - a. The International Marketing Federation?
   - b. International Medical Finance?
   - c. International Maritime Fleets?
   - d. The International Monetary Fund?

3. **What are St Mary's, St Martin's, St Agnes, Bryher and Tresco?**
   Are they:
   - a. French radio stations?
   - b. Bishoprics?
   - c. The Isles of Scilly?
   - d. Islands in the Caribbean?

4. **Who or what is an alewife?**
   Is it:
   - a. A barmaid?
   - b. A female publican?
   - c. Part of the pumping mechanism from the beer barrel to the counter?
   - d. A fish?

5. **What are muniments?**
   Are they:
   - a. Firearms?
   - b. Title deeds?
   - c. Leather leggings?
   - d. Battlements on castle walls?

6. **What do the Scots mean by a 'cuddy'?**
   Is it:
   
       a. A horse or donkey?
       b. A cold in the head?
       c. A cup of tea?
       d. A hug?

7. **Which book is known as the first example of detective fiction in English?**
   Is it:
   
       a. *A Study in Scarlet*?
       b. *The Thirty-nine Steps*?
       c. *The Woman in White*?
       d. *The Moonstone*?

8. **What is mungo?**
   Is it:
   
       a. A fruit?
       b. A fabric?
       c. A language?
       d. A flowing garment?

9. **What is a cos?**
   Is it:
   
       a. An island?
       b. A heavy stick?
       c. A lettuce?
       d. A small lake?

10. **Which country is crossed by both the Equator and the Tropic of Capricorn?**
    Is it:
    
        a. Argentina?
        b. Brazil?
        c. Peru?
        d. Zaire?

# NUMBER, PLEASE

1.  How many years of marriage are celebrated by a sapphire wedding anniversary?
    Is it:

    a. Thirty years?
    b. Forty years?
    c. Forty-five years?
    d. Fifty years?

2.  What total length of beard does the average man shave off in a lifetime?
    Is it:

    a. 500 yards (457 metres)?
    b. 19 miles (31 kilometres)?
    c. 52 miles (84 kilometres)?
    d. 94 miles (151 kilometres)?

3.  What, in degrees Fahrenheit, is 10°C?
    Is it:

    a. 40°F?
    b. 45°F?
    c. 50°F?
    d. 55°F?

4.  How great was the UK's National Debt in 1697?
    Was it:

    a. Nil?
    b. £5,000?
    c. £5,000,000?
    d. £14,000,000?

5.  What percentage of people in Britain own their own houses?
    Is it:

    a. 47%?
    b. 52%?
    c. 63%?
    d. 74%?

6. **What is the population of Manchester?**
   Is it:
   - a. 378,500?
   - b. 457,500?
   - c. 534,000?
   - d. 672,300?

7. **How many universities are there in the UK?**
   Are there:
   - a. Thirty-five?
   - b. Forty-two?
   - c. Forty-six?
   - d. Fifty-two?

8. **What number prime minister of Britain is Margaret Thatcher?**
   Is she:
   - a. The forty-seventh?
   - b. The forty-ninth?
   - c. The fifty-first?
   - d. The fifty-third?

9. **Approximately what is the proportion of cars to people in the USA?**
   Is it:
   - a. One car per four people?
   - b. One car per two people?
   - c. One car per person?
   - d. Two cars per person?

10. **Michael Jackson's album 'Thriller' is the all-time best-selling record to date. Approximately how many copies had it sold by August 1987?**
    Was it:
    - a. 38.5 million?
    - b. 41 million?
    - c. 43.5 million?
    - d. 44.5 million?

# A MIXED BAG

1. **What is a pomade?**
   **Is it:**
   - a. A bunch of flowers?
   - b. The pulpy residue of apples?
   - c. A mixture of aromatic substances?
   - d. Hair dressing?

2. **Where was the Battle of Hastings fought?**
   **Was it at:**
   - a. Hastings?
   - b. Battle?
   - c. Brighton?
   - d. Eastbourne?

3. **What is a theodolite?**
   **Is it:**
   - a. A fossil?
   - b. A surveying instrument?
   - c. A branch of theology?
   - d. A leading priest?

4. **Who wrote *The Compleat Angler*?**
   **Was it:**
   - a. Negley Farson?
   - b. Daniel Farson?
   - c. Rudyard Kipling?
   - d. Isaac Walton?

5. **What is the colour of the Gemini sign of the zodiac?**
   **Is it:**
   - a. Yellow?
   - b. Green?
   - c. Blue?
   - d. Orange?

6. **By what name do Eskimos prefer to be called?**
   **Is it:**
   - a. The People?
   - b. The Dene?
   - c. Inuit?
   - d. Algonquin?

7. **What city has the largest brewery in the world?**
   **Is it:**
   - a. New York?
   - b. Chicago?
   - c. London?
   - d. Dublin?

8. **In sailing terms, what is a droque?**
   **Is it:**
   - a. A contraption to slow down a vessel?
   - b. An extra large jib?
   - c. A three-masted ship?
   - d. A light line with a small weighted bag at the end?

9. **What is narcolepsy?**
   **Is it:**
   - a. A form of epilepsy?
   - b. An addiction to narcotics?
   - c. A sleeping sickness?
   - d. Leprosy?

10. **Which town or city was called Sarum in ancient times?**
    **Was it:**
    - a. Silchester?
    - b. Salisbury?
    - c. Salcombe?
    - d. Shaftesbury?

# THE HIGHWAY CODE

1.  **What is the speed limit of a heavy lorry on a motorway?**
    **Is it:**
    - a. 50 mph?
    - b. 60 mph?
    - c. 65 mph?
    - d. 70 mph?

2.  **What does an amber traffic light mean?**
    **Does it mean:**
    - a. Stop?
    - b. Prepare to stop?
    - c. Prepare to start?
    - d. Proceed with caution?

3.  **What does this road sign mean?**
    **Is it:**

    red triangle
    black bike

    - a. No cycling?
    - b. Cyclists only?
    - c. Cycle route ahead?
    - d. Beware of children?

4.  **When may you *not* overtake on the left?**
    **Is it:**
    - a. When you want to turn left at a junction?
    - b. When traffic is slow moving and vehicles in a lane on the right are moving more slowly than you are?
    - c. When someone is driving slowly on the right of the road looking for a turning?
    - d. In a one-way street?

5.  **What is the speed limit of a car towing a caravan on a dual carriageway?**
    Is it:
    a. 50 mph?
    b. 55 mph?
    c. 60 mph?
    d. 70 mph?

6.  **What should the flashing of headlamps signify?**
    Is it:
    a. A warning to other road users of your presence?
    b. A signal to allow a pedestrian to cross the road in front of you?
    c. A warning to a pedestrian *not* to cross the road in front of you?
    d. A signal to another road user indicating that you are granting them right of way?

7.  **What is the shortest overall stopping distance of a car travelling at 70 mph on a dry road?**
    Is it:
    a. 118 feet (36 metres)?
    b. 175 feet (53 metres)?
    c. 240 feet (73 metres)?
    d. 315 feet (96 metres)?

8.  **What does this road sign mean?**
    Is it:

red circle
black car

    a. No motor vehicles except solo motorcycles, scooters or mopeds?
    b. No cars allowed?
    c. Cars only allowed here?
    d. No parking of cars here?

9.  **If you are driving across an automatic, half-barrier level crossing and amber lights start to flash and a warning sound is heard, what should you do?**
    Should you:
    a. Stop?
    b. Reverse?
    c. Continue?
    d. Get out of the car and run?

10. **What is the speed limit on all roads with street lighting unless signs show otherwise?**
Is it:

  a. 30 mph?
  b. 40 mph?
  c. 50 mph?
  d. 60 mph?

# A MIXED BAG

1. **Where in London is the Royal Shakespeare Company based?**
   Is it at:
   - a. The Royal Court Theatre?
   - b. The Old Vic?
   - c. The Aldwych Theatre?
   - d. The Barbican?

2. **Whose picture appears on the back of a £20 note?**
   Is it:
   - a. The Duke of Wellington's?
   - b. Florence Nightingale's?
   - c. William Shakespeare's?
   - d. Isaac Newton's?

3. **How many polytechnics are there in England and Wales?**
   Are there?
   - a. Twenty?
   - b. Thirty?
   - c. Forty-one?
   - d. Fifty?

4. **What was the nationality of the painter Dante Gabriel Rossetti?**
   Was he:
   - a. British?
   - b. Italian?
   - c. Swiss?
   - d. French?

5. **In which sport is the term *coquille* used?**
   Is it in:
   - a. Lacrosse?
   - b. Skiing?
   - c. Skateboarding?
   - d. Fencing?

6. **Where are the Turks and Caicos Islands?**
   **Are they:**
   - a. Off Florida?
   - d. South-west of Malaysia?
   - c. Near the Bahamas?
   - d. North-west of Fiji?

7. **Why was 'Gilbert' unpopular in September 1988?**
   **Was it because he/it:**
   - a. Devastated the Caribbean?
   - b. Wrote a scurrilous story about the Princess of Wales in the popular press?
   - c. Was a West End play which closed after a week?
   - d. Was a ship loaded with toxic waste that no one wanted in their country?

8. **How many sons and daughters did Queen Victoria have?**
   **Did she have:**
   - a. Four sons and five daughters?
   - b. Five sons and four daughters?
   - c. Six sons and four daughters?
   - d. Three sons and seven daughters?

9. **Which country's people have the longest life expectancy?**
   **Is it the people of:**
   - a. Great Britain?
   - b. The USA?
   - c. Iceland?
   - d. Sweden?

10. **How many cities are there in the United Kingdom?**
    **Are there:**
    - a. 58?
    - b. 123?
    - c. 168?
    - d. 211?

# THE SILVER SCREEN

1.  **What was the very first Dracula film called?**
    **Was it:**
    - a. *Dracula*?
    - b. *Life Without Soul*?
    - c. *Nosferatu*?
    - d. *Dracula, Prince of Darkness*?

2.  **Which famous leading lady starred in these Thirties' films: *Anna Christie, Grand Hotel, Camille*?**
    **Was it:**
    - a. Ginger Rogers?
    - b. Greta Garbo?
    - c. Merle Oberon?
    - d. Bette Davis?

3.  **Who played the man from Laramie in the film of that name?**
    **Was it:**
    - a. Gary Cooper?
    - b. Alan Ladd?
    - c. Roy Rogers?
    - d. James Stewart?

4.  **Who directed *The Last Emperor*?**
    **Was it:**
    - a. Bernardo Bertolucci?
    - b. Steven Spielberg?
    - c. Michael Winner?
    - d. Peter Yates?

5.  **Which was Walt Disney's first full-length cartoon?**
    **Was it:**
    - a. *Pinocchio*?
    - b. *Fantasia*?
    - c. *Bambi*?
    - d. *Snow White and the Seven Dwarfs*?

6. **In which James Bond film did George Lazenby play Bond?**
Was it:

   a. *From Russia With Love*?
   b. *On Her Majesty's Secret Service*?
   c. *Goldfinger*?
   d. *Live and Let Die*?

7. **Which was Marilyn Monroe's last film?**
Was it:

   a. *Bus Stop*?
   b. *The Seven Year Itch*?
   c. *The Prince and the Showgirl*?
   d. *The Misfits*?

8. **In which country did Butch Cassidy and the Sundance Kid end up, in the film of that name?**
Was it:

   a. Mexico?
   b. Bolivia?
   c. Argentina?
   d. Peru?

9. **In which Fifties' musical did Mitzi Gaynor sing 'I'm Gonna Wash That Man Right Out of My Hair'?**
Was it:

   a. *Call Me Madam*?
   b. *South Pacific*?
   c. *The King and I*?
   d. *High Society*?

10. **Who played Annie Hall in the film of that name?**
Was it:

   a. Mia Farrow?
   b. Diane Keaton?
   c. Mariel Hemingway?
   d. Meryl Streep?

# A MIXED BAG

1. **When was the cataclysmic eruption of Krakatoa?**
   **Was it in:**
   - a. 1760?
   - b. 1883?
   - c. 1890?
   - d. 1902?

2. **Which was the first cathedral in Britain to introduce admission charges?**
   **Was it:**
   - a. Worcester?
   - b. Salisbury?
   - c. Wells?
   - d. Ely?

3. **What is a kookaburra?**
   **Is it:**
   - a. A kangaroo?
   - b. A bird?
   - c. A rabbit?
   - d. A shrew?

4. **Which country has the largest investment banking firm in the world?**
   **Is it:**
   - a. Japan?
   - b. Switzerland?
   - c. The USA?
   - d. Great Britain?

5. **How frequently are identical twins born?**
   **Is it:**
   - a. Two sets per thousand births?
   - b. One set per ten thousand births?
   - c. Four sets per thousand births?
   - d. Three sets per hundred births?

6. **What is bronze an alloy of?**
   **Is it:**
   - a. Copper and tin?
   - b. Tin and lead?
   - c. Iron and brass?
   - d. Copper and zinc?

7. **What is a savoy?**
   **Is it:**
   - a. A daisy?
   - b. A smoked sausage?
   - c. A medieval head-dress?
   - d. A cabbage?

8. **What is amber made of?**
   **Is it:**
   - a. Plastic?
   - b. Glass?
   - c. Fossilised resin?
   - d. Dried fruits?

9. **When was the Open University founded?**
   **Was it in:**
   - a. 1960?
   - b. 1965?
   - c. 1969?
   - d. 1972?

10. **Who was the queen of William the Conqueror?**
    **Was she:**
    - a. Maud?
    - b. Matilda?
    - c. Edith?
    - d. Eleanor?

# UNCLE SAM

1. **How many states are there in the USA?**
   **Are there:**
   - a. Forty-eight?
   - b. Forty-nine?
   - c. Fifty?
   - d. Fifty-one?

2. **Which was the first state, admitted to the Union in 1787?**
   **Is it:**
   - a. Connecticut?
   - b. Delaware?
   - c. Pennsylvania?
   - d. New Jersey?

3. **Which state is known as the Blue Grass state?**
   **Is it:**
   - a. Wyoming?
   - b. Vermont?
   - c. Oklahoma?
   - d. Kentucky?

4. **What was the former name of New York?**
   **Was it:**
   - a. St Augustine?
   - b. New Plymouth?
   - c. New London?
   - d. New Amsterdam?

5. **When did the Pilgrim Fathers land in North America?**
   **Was it:**
   - a. 1616?
   - b. 1620?
   - c. 1630?
   - d. 1645?

6. The Mississippi–Missouri is the longest river in the USA. Where does it come in the table of the world's longest rivers?
Is it:
    a. First?
    b. Second?
    c. Third?
    d. Fourth

7. What is the highest mountain in the North American continent?
Is it:
    a. Mount McKinley?
    b. Mount Logan?
    c. King Peak?
    d. Popocatépetl?

8. What was the capital city of America before Washington?
Was it:
    a. Boston?
    b. Philadelphia?
    c. New York?
    d. Albuquerque?

9. Between which dates was the American Civil War fought?
Was it:
    a. 1860–64?
    b. 1861–63?
    c. 1863–65?
    d. 1865–68?

10. Who was president of the USA immediately before Ronald Reagan?
Was it:
    a. Gerald Ford?
    b. Richard Nixon?
    c. Jimmy Carter?
    d. Lyndon Johnson?

# A MIXED BAG

1. **Which county is Hever Castle in?**
   Is it in:
   - a. Kent?
   - b. Sussex?
   - c. Hampshire?
   - d. Dorset?

2. **What is Shanks's pony?**
   Is it:
   - a. A donkey?
   - b. A lame horse or pony?
   - c. A hired horse or pony?
   - d. Travelling on foot?

3. **When was the Domesday Book completed?**
   Was it in:
   - a. 1076?
   - b. 1086?
   - c. 1096?
   - d. 1126?

4. **What does 'chaparral' mean?**
   Is it:
   - a. A mountain range in Spain?
   - b. Dry scrubland, particularly in the south-eastern USA?
   - c. An American saddle horse?
   - d. Leather trousers worn by cowboys?

5. **Who are the Hammers?**
   Are they:
   - a. West Ham United football team?
   - b People who live in Hampstead, north London?
   - c. A New York baseball team?
   - d. A carpenter's union?

6. **What is a clavicle?**
   Is it:
   - a. A collar bone?
   - b. A musical instrument?
   - c. A receptacle for holding holy oil?
   - d. A piece of music played on the harp?

7. **Who was Colley Cibber?**
   Was he:
   - a. A seventeenth-century artist?
   - b. An eighteenth-century Poet Laureate?
   - c. A nineteenth-century architect?
   - d. A 1950s pop star?

8. **Where is Dum Dum Airport?**
   Is it in:
   - a. Malaya?
   - b. China?
   - c. India?
   - d. Pakistan?

9. **What is an eland?**
   Is it:
   - a. A young eel?
   - b. A jutting-out piece of land that is not quite an island?
   - c. A unit of currency?
   - d. An African antelope?

10. **What was Louis Blériot's great achievement?**
    Was he:
    - a. The first man to fly a balloon to the USA?
    - b. The first man to make a powered flight across the English Channel?
    - c. The first man to make a powered flight across the Atlantic?
    - d. The first man to make a powered flight to Australia?

# SPELLING BEE

**Which of the words given in each list are spelt correctly?
What is the correct spelling of those which are incorrect?**

1.
  a. Ambassader.
  b. Beneficence.
  c. Carrillon.
  d. Dalmation.

2.
  a. Espadrille.
  b. Fuschia.
  c. Gynacologist.
  d. Hypocricy.

3.
  a. Jonquil.
  b. Kahki.
  c. Imposter.
  d. Lineament.

4.
  a. Macabre.
  b. Nephritis.
  c. Ommission.
  d. Phthisis.

5.
  a. Querrulous.
  b. Raptor.
  c. Sarsaparilla.
  d. Tobogan.

6.
  a. Urticaria.
  b. Vacination.
  c. Wedgwood.
  d. Xylophone.

7.
    a. Yodell.
    b. Zepellin.
    c. Abhorrent.
    d. Brusque.

8.
    a. Catafalque.
    b. Diarroea.
    c. Entreprener.
    d. Fricasee.

9.
    a. Grafitti.
    b. Heiroglyphic.
    c. Idiosyncracy.
    d. Johdpurs.

10.
    a. Kapock.
    b. Lorgnette.
    c. Ninconpoop.
    d. Machiavellian.

# A MIXED BAG

1. **What is the tapetum?**
   Is it:
   - a. A type of military drum?
   - b. An inflammation in the lining of the stomach?
   - c. A tap-dancing step?
   - d. The part of a cat's eye that apparently glows in the dark?

2. **How many vertebrae are there in a giraffe's neck?**
   Are there:
   - a. Thirty-two?
   - b. Fifty?
   - c. Seven?
   - d. Ten?

3. **During which historical period was the cheese course instituted at dinner?**
   Was it:
   - a. Medieval?
   - b. Stuart?
   - c. Victorian?
   - d. Georgian?

4. **Who illustrated the first published edition of *Alice's Adventures in Wonderland*?**
   Was it:
   - a. Lewis Carroll?
   - b. Kate Greenaway?
   - c. John Tenniel?
   - d. Randolph Caldecott?

5. **Which breed of dog has webbed feet and excels at swimming?**
Is it:
   a. Golden retriever?
   b. Newfoundland?
   c. Gordon setter?
   d. Alsatian?

6. **When were the first state schools introduced in Britain?**
Was it in:
   a. 1870?
   b. 1850?
   c. 1832?
   d. 1905?

7. **What is a sextant?**
Is it:
   a. A group of six vocalists?
   b. An optical navigational instrument?
   c. A church caretaker and bell-ringer?
   d. One of six offspring born at the same time?

8. **Where did the suits of playing cards as we know them probably originate?**
Was it in:
   a. Rouen?
   b. Paris?
   c. Berlin?
   d. Vienna?

9. **What is a pilliwinks?**
Is it:
   a. A medieval instrument of torture?
   b. A child's game?
   c. A sleeping potion with a delayed effect?
   d. A snail that prefers pollution-free soil?

10. **Of what was the mythical Greek Minotaur composed?**
Did it have:
   a. The head of a bull, body of a man?
   b. The head of a boar, body of a horse?
   c. The head of a man, body of a bull?
   d. The head of a man, body of a horse?

# WEAPONS OF WAR

1. **What is a *katana*?**
   Is it:
   - a. A Japanese ensnaring weapon?
   - b. A Chinese pole weapon?
   - c. An oriental foot trap?
   - d. A Japanese long sword?

2. **Who or what was the Gatling gun named after?**
   Was it:
   - a. The ammunition it fired?
   - b. The shape of the butt?
   - c. The inventor?
   - d. The group who financed its development?

3. **When was the matchlock developed?**
   Was it:
   - a. Early in the fifteenth century?
   - b. 1843?
   - c. 1902?
   - d. At the end of the fourteenth century?

4. **The single-edged dagger is called a *kard* in which country?**
   Is it:
   - a. Turkey?
   - b. Saudi Arabia?
   - c. Iran?
   - d. Russia?

5. **When was the tank adopted in Britain?**
   Was it:
   - a. 1935?
   - b. 1900?
   - c. 1915?
   - d. 1922?

6. **Which machine-gun was called the 'Potato Digger'?**
   Was it:
   - a. The Colt-Browning of 1895?
   - b. The German Bergman of 1915?
   - c. The French Darne of 1929?
   - d. The German Parabellum?

7. **During the Second World War, which rifle was mass-produced for use by the British and Commonwealth armies?**
   Was it:
   - a. The American Garand M1?
   - b. The American Carbine M1?
   - c. The Lee-Enfield No. 4?
   - d. The British EM2?

8. **What is a hackbut?**
   Is it:
   - a. A Welsh axe?
   - b. An early Scottish barrel gun?
   - c. A Viking hammer, richly decorated?
   - d. A sixteenth century Norwegian spear?

9. **What is the date of the oldest known Chinese copper gun?**
   Is it AD:
   - a. 1000?
   - b. 1536?
   - c. 1250?
   - d. 1351–2?

10. **In Saudi Arabia, the short, ferociously curved dagger is known by what name?**
    Is it:
    - a. *Yataghan*?
    - b. *Jambiya*?
    - ç. *Shamshu*?
    - d. *Talwar*?

# A MIXED BAG

1. **Which philosopher's ideas form the basis of modern existentialism?**
   Is it:
   - a. Kierkegaard?
   - b. Nietzsche?
   - c. Sartre?
   - d. Schopenhauer?

2. **What is kohl rabi?**
   Is it:
   - a. A cosmetic powder?
   - b. A common language?
   - c. An Ancient Greek dialect?
   - d. A variety of cabbage?

3. **Which athletic events form the women's pentathlon?**
   Are they:
   - a. The 200 metres, the 80 metres hurdles, the shot, the high jump and the long jump?
   - b. The 200 metres, the steeplechase, the discus, the high jump and the long jump?
   - c. The 800 metres, the 100 metres hurdles, the shot, the high jump and the long jump?
   - d. The 400 metres, the 400 metres hurdles, the javelin, the high jump and the long jump?

4. **What nationality was the painter René Magritte?**
   Was he:
   - a. French?
   - b. Belgian?
   - c. Swiss?
   - d. Dutch?

5. **What country is Mogadishu the capital of?**
   Is it:
         a. Morocco?
         b. Mauritania?
         c. Somalia?
         d. Mali?
6. **What is a belvedere?**
   Is it:
         a. An open-sided summer house?
         b. A male deer under three years old?
         c. A note blown on a hunting horn?
         d. Someone employed in forestry?
7. **On which day is the Immaculate Conception of the Blessed Virgin celebrated?**
   Is it on:
         a. 28 March?
         b. 10 April?
         c. 19 September?
         d. 8 December?
8. **What is known as fools' gold?**
   Is it:
         a. Brass?
         b. Citrine?
         c. Iron pyrites?
         d. Mica?
9. **What was Eddie Merckx's sport?**
   Was it:
         a. Running?
         b. Cycling?
         c. Skiing?
         d. Football?
10. **Who wrote books about Mr Jorrocks, the sporting grocer?**
   Was it:
         a. P.G. Wodehouse?
         b. Siegfried Sassoon?
         c. Lewis Carroll?
         d. R.S. Surtees?

# PRIME MINISTERS

1. **How many dukes have been Prime Minister of Great Britain?**
   **Have there been:**
     a. Two?
     b. Five?
     c. Seven?
     d. Nine?

2. **When was Earl Grey Prime Minister?**
   **Was it:**
     a. 1828–30?
     b. 1830–34?
     c. 1852–55?
     d. 1846–52?

3. **How was Sir Archibald Philip Primrose better known?**
   **Was it as:**
     a. The Marquess of Salisbury?
     b. The Earl of Beaconsfield?
     c. The Earl of Rosebery?
     d. Viscount Palmerston?

4. **When Edward Heath was Prime Minister, what was his constituency?**
   **Was it:**
     a. Bexley?
     b. Broadstairs?
     c. Sidcup?
     d. Tunbridge Wells?

5. **Who was Britain's first Labour Prime Minister?**
   **Was it:**
     a. Neville Chamberlain?
     b. Ramsay MacDonald?
     c. Clement Attlee?
     d. Harold Wilson?

6. **Where is Winston Churchill buried?**
   Is it at:
   - a. Blenheim Palace?
   - b. Westminster Abbey?
   - c. Bladon?
   - d. St Paul's Cathedral?

7. **Who was Prime Minister from March 1974 to April 1976?**
   Was it:
   - a. Sir Alec Douglas-Home?
   - b. Harold Wilson?
   - c. Edward Heath?
   - d. Harold Macmillan?

8. **Who was Prime Minister when the king was the uncrowned Edward VIII?**
   Was it:
   - a. Stanley Baldwin?
   - b. Ramsay MacDonald?
   - c. Bonar Law?
   - d. Neville Chamberlain?

9. **How was Lord Dunglass better known?**
   Was it as:
   - a. Anthony Eden?
   - b. Stanley Baldwin?
   - c. Harold Macmillan?
   - d. Alec Douglas-Home?

10. **Who was the first Prime Minister to serve under Queen Elizabeth II?**
    Was it:
    - a. Neville Chamberlain?
    - b. Winston Churchill?
    - c. Clement Attlee?
    - d. Anthony Eden?

# A MIXED BAG

1. **What is a hydrogen clock?**
   Is it:

   a. A digital clock?
   b. A gas-operated clock?
   c. An atomic clock?
   d. A 400-day clock?

2. **Who or what was the mineral alexandrite named after?**
   Was it:

   a. Alexander the Great?
   b. Alexandria?
   c. Tsar Alexander I?
   d. Queen Alexandra?

3. **Why was sea coal so named?**
   Was it because:

   a. It was found under the sea?
   b. It was transported by sea?
   c. It was found on prehistoric seabeds?
   d. It had a high sea-salt content?

4. **Where were cultured pearls first patented?**
   Was it in:

   a. The USA?
   b. Canada?
   c. France?
   d. Japan?

5. **Approximately what percentage of the population is left-handed?**
   Is it:

   a. 1%?
   b. 5%?
   c. 10%?
   d. 25%?

6. **Which country has the oldest continuous parliament in the world?**
   Is it:
   - a. Norway?
   - b. Iceland?
   - c. England?
   - d. The Isle of Man?

7. **Where was gunpowder invented?**
   Was it in:
   - a. China?
   - b. Russia?
   - c. Turkey?
   - d. Japan?

8. **Who is Canada's Head of State?**
   Is it:
   - a. The Prime Minister?
   - b. The Queen?
   - c. The Governor-General?
   - d. The Premier?

9. **In which year was Muhammad Ali the World Heavyweight Champion for the first time?**
   Was it:
   - a. 1959?
   - b. 1964?
   - c. 1967?
   - d. 1970?

10. **What is a mud puppy?**
    Is it:
    - a. An excitable young dog?
    - b. A fish?
    - c. A bird?
    - d. A salamander?

# GARDENERS' WORLD

1. **Which pH value of soil represents a neutral balance between acidity and alkalinity?**
   Is it:
   
   a. 6?
   b. 7?
   c. 9?
   d. 12?

2. **What colour is the rose 'Peace'?**
   Is it:
   
   a. White?
   b. White, tinted with pink?
   c. Cream?
   d. Yellow, edged with pink?

3. **'Scarlet Emperor' is a popular variety of what?**
   Is it:
   
   a. A tomato?
   b. A potato?
   c. An onion?
   d. A runner bean?

4. **Which of the following flowers is *not* a perennial?**
   Is it:
   
   a. A hosta?
   b. A forget-me-not?
   c. Love-in-a-mist?
   d. A Michaelmas daisy?

5. **What are Beauty of Bath, Worcester Pearmain and James Grieve?**
   Are they:
   
   a. Early dessert apples?
   b. Late dessert apples?
   c. Early dessert pears?
   d. Dessert plums?

6. **Which flowers are red, pink or white on lime soils, and blue or lilac on acid soils?**
   Are they those of the:
   - a. Rhododendron?
   - b. Peony?
   - c. Hydrangea?
   - d. Hyacinth?

7. **What is a pelargonium better known as?**
   Is it a:
   - a. Lily?
   - b. Poppy?
   - c. Solomon's Seal?
   - d. Geranium?

9. **What colour is a ceanothus?**
   Is it:
   - a. Blue?
   - b. Red?
   - c. Yellow?
   - d. White?

9. **What are leatherjackets?**
   Are they:
   - a. Dung-eating beetles?
   - b. Centipedes?
   - c. The larvae of crane flies?
   - d. Cabbage-white caterpillars?

10. **What are Montana, Nelly Moser, Hagley Hybrid and Jackmanii Superba?**
    Are they varieties of:
    - a. Wisteria?
    - b. Clematis?
    - c. Honeysuckle?
    - d. Magnolia?

1. **What is the gauge of Britain's railways?**
   **Is it:**
   - a. 4 ft 8½ ins?
   - b. 5 ft 4½ ins?
   - c. 6 ft?
   - d. 6 ft 6 ins?

2. **What is Proxima Centauri?**
   **Is it:**
   - a. The nearest group of stars to the Earth?
   - b. A primitive water-dwelling organism?
   - c. A pop group?
   - d. An ancestor of the present horse?

3. **Which beetle must be reported to the Ministry of Agriculture if seen in Britain?**
   **Is it the:**
   - a. Powder post beetle?
   - b. Death-watch beetle?
   - c. Longhorn beetle?
   - d. Colorado beetle?

4. **Who would use a wok?**
   **Would it be:**
   - a. A cook?
   - b. A pilot?
   - c. A carpenter?
   - d. A surgeon?

5. **When did the Wright brothers make the first flight in a petrol-powered aeroplane?**
   **Was it in:**
   - a. 1897?
   - b. 1903?
   - c. 1919?
   - d. 1925?

6.  **What game does Sue Barker play?**
    **Is it:**
    - a. Tennis?
    - b. Golf?
    - c. Badminton?
    - d. Hockey?

7.  **Where is the island of Hoy?**
    **Is it in:**
    - a. The Outer Hebrides?
    - b. The Faeroes?
    - c. Orkney?
    - d. Shetland?

8.  **Who was Dandini?**
    **Was he:**
    - a. Widow Twankey's son?
    - b. Prince Charming's valet?
    - c. Dick Whittington's cat?
    - d. Ali Baba's chief thief?

9.  **What is Chris Bonington famous for?**
    **Is he:**
    - a. A best-selling author?
    - b. Chairman of the Austin-Rover group?
    - c. A mountaineer?
    - d. A violinist?

10. **What kind of feather was a quill pen traditionally made from?**
    **Was it:**
    - a. Duck?
    - b. Goose?
    - c. Hen?
    - d. Swan?

# PETS' CORNER

1. **Where do budgerigars come from?**
   Is it:
   - a. South Africa?
   - b. Australia?
   - c. India?
   - d. Argentina?

2. **Which of the following breeds of dog was not originally bred as a sheepdog?**
   Is it:
   - a. The Alsatian?
   - b. The Corgi?
   - c. The Cocker Spaniel?
   - d. The Rottweiler?

3. **What is a Belgian hare?**
   Is it:
   - a. A hare?
   - b. A rabbit?
   - c. A hamster?
   - d. A guinea pig?

4. **In which kind of country does a gerbil live in its natural habitat?**
   Is it:
   - a. The desert?
   - b. Thickly wooded country?
   - c. Grassland?
   - d. Water meadows?

5. **Where do canaries come from?**
   Is it?
   - a. The Canary Islands?
   - b. The West Indies?
   - c. Ecuador?
   - d. Fiji?

6. **What colour is the Havana cat?**
   Is it:
   - a. Black?
   - b. White?
   - c. Biscuit-coloured with darker 'points'?
   - d. Chestnut brown?

7. **What is the average lifespan of a hamster?**
   Is it:
   - a. Less than one year?
   - b. Not more than three or four years, and often less?
   - c. Up to five years?
   - d. Up to eight years?

8. **What is an axolotl?**
   Is it:
   - a. A fish?
   - b. A type of newt?
   - c. A snake?
   - d. The young of a salamander?

9. **What is the minimum amount of exercise a medium-sized dog such as a Labrador needs daily?**
   Is it:
   - a. 3 miles (5 kilometres)?
   - b. 6 miles (9½ kilometres)?
   - c. 9 miles (14 kilometres)?
   - d. 12 miles (19 kilometres)?

10. **What kind of pet is a Maine Coon?**
    Is it:
    - a. A dog?
    - b. A cat?
    - c. A raccoon?
    - d. A rabbit?

# A MIXED BAG

1. **What is magma?**
   Is it:
   - a. A grey metal which cannot be magnetised?
   - b. The non-fat part of milk?
   - c. The molten fluid within the Earth's crust?
   - d. A trimming made by knotting threads?

2. **How many clubs are there in a set of golf clubs?**
   Are there?
   - a. Eight?
   - b. Ten?
   - c. Twelve?
   - d. Fourteen?

3. **The Temple of Artemis was one of the Seven Wonders of the Ancient World. Where was it?**
   Was it at:
   - a. Alexandria?
   - b. Babylon?
   - c. Ephesus?
   - d. Rhodes?

4. **What was the first American space shuttle called?**
   Was it:
   - a. Apollo?
   - b. Columbia?
   - c. Skylab?
   - d. Gemini?

5. **When was Pope John Paul II elected?**
   Was it in:
   - a. 1976?
   - b. 1978?
   - c. 1980?
   - d. 1982?

6. **What is humus?**
   **Is it:**
   - a. A creamy dip made from chick peas?
   - b. Another word for humidity?
   - c. Partially decomposed matter?
   - d. A note produced by a bell when struck?

7. **Buddhism is based on the teaching of an Indian prince. What was his name?**
   **Was it:**
   - a. Brahma?
   - b. Vishnu?
   - c. Shiva?
   - d. Siddhartha?

8. **What was *Der Blaue Reiter*?**
   **Was it:**
   - a. A steam locomotive?
   - b. A group of Expressionist painters?
   - c. A classic 1930s film?
   - d. A German postage stamp?

9. **Where is the Celebes Sea?**
   **Is it:**
   - a. East of Borneo?
   - b. East of New Guinea?
   - c. South-east of Australia?
   - d. Between Mozambique and Madagascar?

10. **In which sport might you come across the word 'salchow'?**
    **Would it be concerned with:**
    - a. Swimming?
    - b. Skating?
    - c. Karate?
    - d. Bob-sleighing?

# FOREIGN WORDS AND PHRASES

**What do the foreign words and phrases in these questions mean?**

1. *In camera*
   - a. Revealed by a photograph.
   - b. In private, or in secret.
   - c. Packed in a box.
   - d. In friendship.

2. *Hoi polloi*
   - a. A hunting cry.
   - b. A lot of nonsense.
   - c. The majority, the masses.
   - d. At break of day.

3. *Savoire-faire*
   - a. Well-bred.
   - b. Well-read.
   - c. Tact.
   - d. Gourmet tastes.

4. *Bitte nehmen Sie Platz*
   - a. Can you direct me to the square?
   - b. Please queue this side.
   - c. No ball games allowed here.
   - d. Please sit down.

5. *Hasta la vista*
   - a. I'll be seeing you.
   - b. Look at the view.
   - c. Time rushes by.
   - d. Through the window.

6. *Sine qua non*
   - a. It goes without saying.
   - b. An indispensable condition or qualification.
   - c. A pen-name.
   - d. A nod of the head.

7. *Perchè*
    a. Perching.
    b. Fish.
    c. A pearl.
    d. Why?
8. *Fait accompli*
    a. A partner in crime.
    b. Something done and no longer worth worrying about.
    c. An accomplished artist.
    d. A major work.
9. *Frisch gestrichen*
    a. Fresh air.
    b. Fresh vegetables.
    c. Wet paint.
    d. A strict diet.
10. *Come sta?*
    a. Come here.
    b. Which way is the station?
    c. Like this?
    d. How do you do?

# A MIXED BAG

1. **What is the world's tallest free-standing structure?**
   **Is it:**
   - a. The Post Office Tower in London?
   - b. The Television Tower in Ostankino, USSR?
   - c. The Eiffel Tower in Paris?
   - d. The CN Tower in Toronto?

2. **What is jet?**
   **Is it:**
   - a. Lignite?
   - b. Vulcanite?
   - c. Bakelite?
   - d. Glass?

3. **What is an albert?**
   **Is it:**
   - a. A kind of WC?
   - b. A watch chain?
   - c. A hat?
   - d. A carriage?

4. **How is maple syrup obtained?**
   **Is it made from:**
   - a. Crushed maple leaves?
   - b. Crushed fruits from maple trees?
   - c. Liquid tapped from maple trees?
   - d. A synthetic substance and sugar syrup?

5. **Who wrote *The Water Babies*?**
   **Was it:**
   - a. Sir Arthur Conan Doyle?
   - b. Charles Kingsley?
   - c. Robert Louis Stevenson?
   - d. Rider Haggard?

6. **When was the fairy tale *Cinderella* first told?**
   Was it:
   
   a. At least 1000 years ago?
   b. 1588?
   c. 1851?
   d. 1901?

7. **What is carnival glass?**
   Is it:
   
   a. Glass used by circus people?
   b. Antique irridescent glass?
   c. Colourfully striped glass?
   d. Fairy lights?

8. **Which man-made structure can be seen from outer space?**
   Is it:
   
   a. Hadrian's Wall?
   b. The Great Wall of China?
   c. The Rockefeller Centre in New York?
   d. The Sydney Opera House?

9. **What was a *claddagh* ring?**
   Was it:
   
   a. An Irish engagement ring?
   b. A Scottish clan ring?
   c. A signet ring, set with a stone?
   d. A collection of Irish farmers at a cattle auction?

10. **What is the specific gravity of gold?**
    Is it:
    
    a. 15?
    b. 18.9?
    c. 19.3?
    d. 21.4?

# THE WILD, WILD WEST

1.  **Which famous Western character named the place in which he settled Langtry, in honour of the actress Lillie Langtry?**
    Was it:

    a. 'Wild Bill' Hickok?
    b. Judge Roy Bean?
    c. Wyatt Earp?
    d. Pat Garrett?

2.  **What was a 'prairie schooner'?**
    Was it:

    a. A large covered wagon?
    b. A horse saddled with Western gear?
    c. A large glass out of which whisky was drunk?
    d. A pot for brewing coffee?

3.  **What connects Jim Bowie, Davy Crockett and William Travis?**
    Did they:

    a. All die defending the Alamo?
    b. All hunt Billy the Kid?
    c. All get hanged as murderers?
    d. All invent weapons?

4.  **For how long did the Pony Express operate?**
    Was it:

    a. For eighteen months?
    b. For two and a half years?
    c. For five years?
    d. For ten years?

5. **What were the *Henry Frank*, the *Natchez* and the *Robert E. Lee*?**
   Were they:
   - a. Steam locomotives?
   - b. Stage coaches?
   - c. Mississippi riverboats?
   - d. Trading posts?

6. **Which of the following was not a Sioux chief?**
   - a. Sitting Bull?
   - b. Black Kettle?
   - c. Crazy Horse?
   - d. Red Cloud?

7. **When was Custer's Last Stand?**
   Was it in:
   - a. 1856?
   - b. 1866?
   - c. 1876?
   - d. 1886?

8. **What was a 'maverick'?**
   Was it:
   - a. Someone who cheated at cards?
   - b. An unbranded calf?
   - c. A gun that fired only one shot?
   - d. An unruly cowboy?

9. **Which robber gang came to a spectacular end in Coffeyville, Kansas?**
   Was it:
   - a. Frank and Jesse James and their men?
   - b. The Youngers?
   - c. The Daltons?
   - d. Butch Cassidy and the Sundance Kid?

10. **What was the 'remuda'?**
    Was it:
    - a. Another name for a cattle ranch?
    - b. The stock of riding horses from which cowboys selected their mounts?
    - c. The roll of belongings (bedroll, etc.) that a cowboy carried on his saddle?
    - d. The name given to the time when a cowboy was out on the trail, herding cattle?

# A MIXED BAG

1. **If a car carries the registration letters GBZ, where does it come from?**
   Is it:
   - a. Northern Ireland?
   - b. Hong Kong?
   - c. The Isle of Man?
   - d. Gibraltar?

2. **What is a *doppelganger*?**
   Is it:
   - a. A double attempt at something?
   - b. An apparition of a living person?
   - c. A man who mends the roads?
   - d. A small dessert apple?

3. **What is Mstislav Rostropovich's instrument?**
   Is it:
   - a. The violin?
   - b. The cello?
   - c. The piano?
   - d. The harpsichord?

4. **When did the South Sea Bubble burst?**
   Was it:
   - a. In 1701?
   - b. In 1720?
   - c. In 1740?
   - d. In 1759?

5. **Which 'firth' does Edinburgh stand on?**
   Is it:
   - a. The Firth of Forth?
   - b. The Firth of Tay?
   - c. The Moray Firth?
   - d. The Firth of Clyde?

6. **What is the Earth's smallest continent?**
   **Is it:**
   - a. Australia?
   - b. Antarctica?
   - c. Africa?
   - d. Europe?

7. **When was the Aberfan disaster?**
   **Was it in:**
   - a. 1962?
   - b. 1966?
   - c. 1968?
   - d. 1970?

8. **What is the littoral?**
   **Is it:**
   - a. The shoreline?
   - b. The seashore between low and high tide?
   - c. A printer's error?
   - d. A story passed on verbally?

9. **How many bones are there in the human arm?**
   **Are there:**
   - a. Twelve?
   - b. Twenty?
   - c. Thirty?
   - d. Forty?

10. **What is a saluki?**
    **Is it:**
    - a. A Russian drink?
    - b. A small cigar?
    - c. A water channel in Roman baths?
    - d. A breed of dog?

# ART AND ARTISTS

1. **Who painted *La Primavera*?**
   **Was it:**
   - a. Leonardo da Vinci?
   - b. Filippo Lippi?
   - c. Sandro Botticelli?
   - d. Antonio Canaletto?

2. **What was Grinling Gibbons's art?**
   **Was it:**
   - a. Engraving?
   - b. Sculpting?
   - c. Painting?
   - d. Woodcarving?

3. **Which animals was Théodore Géricault famous for painting?**
   **Were they:**
   - a. Horses?
   - b. Dogs?
   - c. Farm animals?
   - d. Cats?

4. **His earliest major work was the *North Wind* (1928) commissioned for the London Underground building. Who was he?**
   **Was he:**
   - a. Eric Gill?
   - b. Henry Moore?
   - c. Paul Klee?
   - d. Alberto Giacometti?

5. **Who painted the *Laughing Cavalier*?**
   **Was it:**
   - a. Goya?
   - b. Van Dyck?
   - c. Rembrandt?
   - d. Franz Hals?

6. **Who was the first artist to be the subject of two biographies in his lifetime?**
   Was he:
   - a. Michelangelo?
   - b. Leonardo da Vinci?
   - c. Giotto?
   - d. Raphael?

7. **Which of the following artists was a famous watercolourist?**
   Was it:
   - a. Graham Sutherland?
   - b. Jean Watteau?
   - c. John Sell Cotman?
   - d. Wilson Steer?

8. **What is the name of a portrait measuring 36 × 28 inches, showing the head and one hand?**
   Is it called:
   - a. A cartoon?
   - b. A miniature?
   - c. A Kit-cat?
   - d. A tondo?

9. **He was 'the most productive and celebrated designer of wood-engraved book illustrations of the nineteenth century' and was famous for those depicting the squalor of life in London. Who was he?**
   Was he:
   - a. Thomas Bewick?
   - b. Gustave Doré?
   - c. Thomas Rowlandson?
   - d. William Hogarth?

10. **What does the term *sfumato* mean?**
    Is it:
    - a. Imperceptible transitions of tone from light to dark?
    - b. A technique in which coloured plaster is placed over white plaster and then scratched off to reveal a design?
    - c. A technique in which tiny dots of primary colours apparently combine to form new colours?
    - d. The skill with which a painter depicts shadows?

# A MIXED BAG

1. **Which country is the oldest kingdom?**
   Is it:
   - a. Denmark?
   - b. Iceland?
   - c. Swaziland?
   - d. Great Britain?

2. **Which planet is nearest to the Sun?**
   Is it:
   - a. Venus?
   - b. Mercury?
   - c. Mars?
   - d. Saturn?

3. **Where was the first toilet built in a private house in England?**
   Was it:
   - a. Blenheim Palace?
   - b. The Mansion House?
   - c. Ham House?
   - d. Paycocke's?

4. **Who discovered the speed of light?**
   Was it:
   - a. Ole Rømer?
   - b. Sir Karl Popper?
   - c. Thomas Jefferson?
   - d. Talleyrand?

5. **What name was Australia first given by the Europeans?**
   Was it:
   - a. Tasmania?
   - b. New Caledonia?
   - c. New Holland?
   - d. Green Land?

6. **In which town is the National Library of Wales?**
   **Is it:**
   - a. Aberystwyth?
   - b. Cardiff?
   - c. Llandrindod Wells?
   - d. Brecon?

7. **Where was Danish pastry first made?**
   **Was it in:**
   - a. Paris?
   - b. Copenhagen?
   - c. Vienna?
   - d. Lucerne?

8. **When was *Star Trek* first shown on TV?**
   **Was it:**
   - a. 1968?
   - b. 1965?
   - c. 1980?
   - d. 1971?

9. **Who was the general on the winning side at the Battle of Copenhagen?**
   **Was it:**
   - a. Wolfe?
   - b. Nelson?
   - c. de Groote?
   - d. Montcalm?

10. **What did Gandhi do when he lived in London as a young man?**
    **Was he:**
    - a. A medical student?
    - b. A gardener at Buckingham Palace?
    - c. A teacher in a school for handicapped children?
    - d. Kitchen staff at the Savoy?

# THE RULES OF THE GAME

1. **How long is a netball pitch?**
   Is it:
   - a. 18.3 metres (60 feet)?
   - b. 24.4 metres (80 feet)?
   - c. 30.5 metres (100 feet)?
   - d. 36.5 metres (120 feet)?

2. **How many points is a try worth in rugby?**
   Is it:
   - a. One point?
   - b. Two points?
   - c. Three points?
   - d. Four points?

3. **What colour belt does a beginner in karate wear?**
   Is it:
   - a. White?
   - b. Red?
   - c. Blue?
   - d. Green?

4. **What is the line 1.22 metres (4 feet) in front of the bowling crease on a cricket pitch called?**
   Is it called:
   - a. The gully?
   - b. The slips?
   - c. Mid-wicket?
   - d. The popping crease?

5. **When a free kick is taken in soccer, how far from the ball must the opposing players be?**
   Is it at least:
   - a. 9 metres (10 yards)?
   - b. 11 metres (12 yards)?
   - c. 13 metres (14 yards)?
   - d. 13.7 metres (15 yards)?

6. **In tennis, who wins the game when a tie break is used?**
Is it:
   - a. The first player to reach six points with a one-point lead?
   - b. The first player to reach six points with a two-point lead?
   - c. The first player to reach seven points with a one-point lead?
   - d. The first player to reach seven points with a two-point lead?

7. **What is the maximum number of feathers in a shuttlecock in a game of badminton?**
Is it:
   - a. Twelve?
   - b. Sixteen?
   - c. Twenty?
   - d. Twenty-four?

8. **What marks the bases, other than the home base, in baseball?**
Is it:
   - a. White posts?
   - b. White crosses on the ground?
   - c. Red and white flags?
   - d. White canvas bags?

9. **In which game is the playing field known as the gridiron?**
Is it:
   - a. Baseball?
   - b. American football?
   - c. Australian football?
   - d. Lacrosse?

10. **Put these weights of boxers in ascending order, starting with the lightest.**
   - a. Lightweight.
   - b. Light welterweight.
   - c. Bantamweight.
   - d. Featherweight.

# A MIXED BAG

1.  **What is the capital of Nigeria?**
    Is it:
    - a. Dar es Salaam?
    - b. Luanda?
    - c. Lusaka?
    - d. Lagos?
2.  **What is the IAAF?**
    Is it:
    - a. The Institute of Amalgamated Armourers and Firemen?
    - b. The Incorporated Association of Amateur Fishermen?
    - c. The International Amateur Athletic Federation?
    - d. The International Amateur Aviation Federation?
3.  **What is the English name for Mardi Gras?**
    Is it:
    - a. Whitsuntide?
    - b. Shrove Tuesday?
    - c. Ash Wednesday?
    - d. May Day?
4.  **What does the spleen do?**
    Does it:
    - a. Produce white blood cells?
    - b. Produce red blood cells?
    - c. Produce insulin?
    - d. Produce digestive enzymes?
5.  **Who was the first man on the Moon?**
    Was it:
    - a. Neil Armstrong?
    - b. Buzz Aldrin?
    - c. Michael Collins?
    - d. Alan Shephard?

6. **How many stripes are there on the American flag?**
   **Are there:**
   - a. Thirteen?
   - b. Nineteen?
   - c. Twenty-five?
   - d. Fifty?

7. **What money would you use in Egypt?**
   **Would it be:**
   - a. The dirham?
   - b. The Egyptian dollar?
   - c. The Egyptian pound?
   - d. The Egyptian dinar?

8. **What is a 'bird' in badminton?**
   **Is it:**
   - a. A wide hit?
   - b. A missed hit?
   - c. A shuttlecock?
   - d. A type of racket?

9. **Where is Leonardo da Vinci airport?**
   **Is it in:**
   - a. Rome?
   - b. Milan?
   - c. Venice?
   - d. Pisa?

10. **Where is Waverley railway station?**
    **Is it in:**
    - a. Liverpool?
    - b. Manchester?
    - c. Birmingham?
    - d. Edinburgh?

# ·OLOGIES

'. . . ology' means a study of something. What are the
following words studies of?

1. **Arthrology?**
   Is it:
   - a. Blood vessels?
   - b. Spiders?
   - c. Joints?
   - d. Skills?

2. **Bryology?**
   Is it:
   - a. Aquatic animals?
   - b. Food?
   - c. Climbing plants?
   - d. Mosses?

3. **Carcinology?**
   Is it:
   - a. Crustaceans?
   - b. Tumours?
   - c. The heart?
   - d. Coal?

4. **Demology?**
   Is it:
   - a. Skin?
   - b. Human activities?
   - c. The devil?
   - d. Ancient writing?

5. **Enterology?**
   Is it:
   - a. Insects?
   - b. Thermal energy?
   - c. Doors and doorways?
   - d. Internal parts?

6. **Hydrology?**
   **Is it:**
   - a. The growing of plants without soil?
   - b. Water?
   - c. The Earth's contours?
   - d. Sleep?

7. **Palaeontology?**
   **Is it:**
   - a. The past history of life?
   - b. Fossilised fish?
   - c. The human brain?
   - d. Universal knowledge?

8. **Pyrology?**
   **Is it:**
   - a. The stomach?
   - b. Fevers?
   - c. Towers?
   - d. Fire and heat?

9. **Pedology?**
   **Is it:**
   - a. Feet?
   - b. Teaching?
   - c. Soils?
   - d. Lice?

10. **Tidology?**
   **Is it:**
   - a. Tides?
   - b. Values?
   - c. Postage stamps?
   - d. Miracles?

# A MIXED BAG

1. **When was David Livingstone born?**
   **Was it:**
   - a. 1789?
   - b. 1813?
   - c. 1825?
   - d. 1833?

2. **What is a baby kangaroo called?**
   **Is it:**
   - a. A cub?
   - b. A calf?
   - c. A harry?
   - d. A joey?

3. **Why is breadfruit so named?**
   **Is it because:**
   - a. It looks like bread?
   - b. It tastes like bread?
   - c. It has a texture like bread?
   - d. A type of bread can be made from it?

4. **Who was Richard Cobden?**
   **Was he:**
   - a. An English economist and statesman?
   - b. A composer of operettas?
   - c. A teacher and author?
   - d. An early union leader?

5. **What is the Coal Sack?**
   **Is it:**
   - a. The seat of the Lord Chancellor in the House of Lords?
   - b. The symbol of the National Union of Mineworkers?
   - c. A dark nebula in the Milky Way?
   - d. A famous pub in Newcastle?

6. **On the coast of which sea is Sevastopol?**
Is it on:
   a. The Black Sea?
   b. The Caspian Sea?
   c. The Sea of Marmara?
   d. The Aegean Sea?

7. **What is HMS *Belfast*, near London's Tower Bridge, used for?**
Is it:
   a. A museum?
   b. A restaurant?
   c. A rescue ship?
   d. A functioning naval vessel?

8. **Where was the Crystal Palace built for the Great Exhibition of 1851?**
Was it in:
   a. Hackney Marshes?
   b. Richmond Park?
   c. Hyde Park?
   d. Green Park?

9. **Who opened the National Theatre in 1976?**
Was it:
   a. The Queen Mother?
   b. The Queen?
   c. Sir Laurence Olivier?
   d. Princess Margaret?

10. **What structure on Monte Cassino was bombed in 1944?**
Was it:
   a. A hospital run by nuns?
   b. A Franciscan school?
   c. A Trappist monastery?
   d. A Benedictine monastery?

# DOWN BY THE RIVER

1. **What is the longest navigable river in the world?**
   Is it:
   - a. The Amazon?
   - b. The Nile?
   - c. The Mississippi?
   - d. The Yellow River?

2. **What is the longest river in the British Isles?**
   Is it:
   - a. The Severn?
   - b. The Thames?
   - c. The Shannon?
   - d. The Tay?

3. **Which Australian city is on the Parramatta River?**
   Is it:
   - a. Adelaide?
   - b. Melbourne?
   - c. Perth?
   - d. Sydney?

4. **Which river reaches the sea at Leningrad?**
   Is it:
   - a. The Volga?
   - b. The Don?
   - c. The Neva?
   - d. The Unzha?

5. **Which river flows through Florence?**
   Is it:
   - a. The Volturno?
   - b. The Arno?
   - c. The Po?
   - d. The Tiber?

6. **What city is at the mouth of the Yangtze Kiang?**
   Is it:
   - a. Peking?
   - b. Shanghai?
   - c. Hanoi?
   - d. Hangchow?

7. **Which one of the following cities does the Nile *not* flow through?**
   Is it:
   - a. Cairo?
   - b. Aswan?
   - c. Addis Ababa?
   - d. Khartoum?

8. **Where do the Mississippi and Missouri join?**
   Is it at:
   - a. St Louis?
   - b. Memphis?
   - c. Minneapolis?
   - d. Omaha?

9. **Which great French river flows to the sea through Nantes?**
   Is it:
   - a. The Garonne?
   - b. The Lot?
   - c. The Loire?
   - d. The Dordogne?

10. **On which American river is the Grand Canyon?**
    Is it on:
    - a. The Rio Grande?
    - b. The Colorado?
    - c. The Snake?
    - d. The South Platte?

# A MIXED BAG

1.  **Which is the biggest lake in the world (excluding seas)?**
    Is it:
        a. Lake Superior?
        b. Lake Victoria?
        c. Lake Huron?
        d. Lake Michigan?

2.  **Where does pumice come from?**
    Does it come from:
        a. A volcano?
        b. The sea?
        c. River beds?
        d. A quarry in southern Italy?

3.  **What do the letters SALT stand for?**
    Is it:
        a. The Society for the Upholding of Artistic and Literary Traditions?
        b. Strategic Arms Limitation Talks?
        c. Southern Administration, London Transport?
        d. South American Linguistics Trust?

4.  **When did Mikhail Gorbachev become President of the USSR?**
    Was it in:
        a. October 1984?
        b. March 1985?
        c. November 1985?
        d. February 1986?

5.  **Who composed the opera *Hansel and Gretel*?**
    Was it:
        a. Engelbert Humperdinck?
        b. Beethoven?
        c. Mahler?
        d. Haydn?

6. **What is, or was, the Koh-i-nor?**
   Was/is it:
     a. A mountain range in India?
     b. A mountain range in South Africa?
     c. A diamond in the British Crown Jewels?
     d. An Indian nobleman?

7. **When was Offa's Dyke built?**
   Was it approximately:
     a. 45 BC?
     b. AD 500?
     c. AD 290?
     d. AD 785?

8. **How many nails are there traditionally in a horseshoe?**
     a. Five?
     b. Six?
     c. Seven?
     d. Eight?

9. **What is a galliard?**
   Is it:
     a. A short decorative sword?
     b. A lively dance?
     c. An eighteenth-century dandy?
     d. Part of a ship's rigging?

10. **What is a Turkish Van?**
    Is it:
     a. A camel?
     b. A civic official?
     c. A breed of cat?
     d. A type of sweetmeat?

# ROMAN BRITAIN

1. **Which one of the following is *not* a Roman road?**
   Is it:
   - a. Fosse Way?
   - b. Ridge Way?
   - c. Stane Street?
   - d. Watling Street?

2. **Where are there ruins of a Roman villa which is believed to have been larger than Nero's palace in Rome?**
   Is it:
   - a. London?
   - b. Fishbourne?
   - c. York?
   - d. Bognor?

3. **When was Hadrian's Wall built?**
   Was it:
   - a. AD 100–150?
   - b. 50 BC–AD 100?
   - c. AD 300–320?
   - d. AD 120–123?

4. **Where is the site of Roman Verulamium?**
   Is it:
   - a. Near St Albans?
   - b. North of Peterborough?
   - c. Silchester?
   - d. Near Winchester?

5. **Where is the supposed landing spot for the main Roman invasion of England?**
   Is it:
   - a. Chichester?
   - b. Richborough?
   - c. Hythe?
   - d. Dover?

6. **Where in England does a Roman pharos or lighthouse still stand?**
   Is at at:
   - a. Brighton?
   - b. Reculver?
   - c. Bradwell-on-Sea?
   - d. Dover?

7. **Why were the troops at the Roman fort at Pevensey Castle and the nine other Roman shore forts recalled to Rome?**
   Was it because:
   - a. There was an acute shortage of food?
   - b. Rome was sacked by the Goths?
   - c. The local people rose up against them?
   - d. Rome was planning an invasion of North Africa?

8. **Where does a plaque mark the spot where Julius Caesar reputedly landed in Britain?**
   Is it at:
   - a. Barfreston?
   - b. Deal?
   - c. Dover?
   - d. Folkestone?

9. **When was the great Roman city of Colchester sacked by Boadicea?**
   Was it:
   - a. 10 BC?
   - b. 32 BC?
   - c. AD 52?
   - d. AD 60?

10. **Why did the Romans found Londinium (London) soon after AD 43?**
    Was it because:
    - a. The soil was particularly well suited to planting vineyards?
    - b. The priests chose the most auspicious spot in the most auspicious year?
    - c. It was the furthest point up the Thames ships could sail on the tide?
    - d. It was exactly 100 days' journey from Rome?

**A MIXED BAG**

1. **Who composed the opera *Rigoletto*?**
   Was it:
   - a. Rachmaninoff?
   - b. Giuseppe Verdi?
   - c. Beethoven?
   - d. Benjamin Britten?

2. **Where was the county of Radnorshire before the reorganisation in 1974?**
   Was it in:
   - a. North Yorkshire?
   - b. Cumbria?
   - c. Dumfriesshire?
   - d. East Wales?

3. **What does Rafferty's Rules mean?**
   Is it:
   - a. A code for boxing?
   - b. Rules for a card game?
   - c. An unwritten code of behaviour for rugby?
   - d. No rules?

4. **In what year was the Magna Carta granted by King John at Runnymede?**
   Was it:
   - a. 1305?
   - b. 1410?
   - c. 1215?
   - d. 1398?

5. **What is the solar plexus?**
   Is it:
   - a. The base of the neck?
   - b. A network of nerves?
   - c. The 'funny bone' in the elbow?
   - d. The small toe?

6. **Where is the Matterhorn?**
   **Is it:**
   - a. On the border between Italy and Switzerland?
   - b. In Austria?
   - c. On the border between Austria and Switzerland?
   - d. In Switzerland?

7. **What does solecism mean?**
   **Is it:**
   - a. Rhyming words?
   - b. Non-standard use of grammar?
   - c. Confusing words with a similar sound?
   - d. A word that mimics the sound or action of what it is describing?

8. **What is the capital of Tanzania?**
   **Is it:**
   - a. Zanzibar?
   - b. Dar es Salaam?
   - c. Morogoro?
   - d. Mombasa?

9. **When were the Dark Ages?**
   **Were they from approximately:**
   - a. AD 400 to AD 1000?
   - b. 100 BC to AD 500?
   - c. 1000 BC to AD 500?
   - d. 600 BC to AD 400?

10. **What is a madeleine?**
    **Is it:**
    - a. A musical instrument similar to a lyre?
    - b. A head-dress?
    - c. A dish containing a number of ingredients?
    - d. A small fancy sponge cake?

# COME RAIN, COME SHINE

1. **Where is the wettest place in the world?**
   Is it in:
   - a. Burma?
   - b. Hawaii?
   - c. The Brazilian rain forest?
   - d. Borneo?

2. **In which direction does the *mistral* blow?**
   Is it from:
   - a. The north?
   - b. The south?
   - c. The east?
   - d. The west?

3. **What is St Elmo's fire?**
   Is it:
   - a. The light seen round the edge of the sun when it is in eclipse?
   - b. A glowing sphere of lightning?
   - c. A fire started by the sun shining on a lens?
   - d. A discharge of static electricity around the tips of tall objects?

4. **When was the last white Christmas in London?**
   Was it in:
   - a. 1970?
   - b. 1978?
   - c. 1981?
   - d. 1985?

5. **During which months does the monsoon occur in south-east Asia?**
   Is it between:
   - a. April and December?
   - b. August and January?
   - c. October and March?
   - d. December and June?

6. **What is described as force ten on the Beaufort Scale?**
   Is it:

       a. A fresh breeze?
       b. A gale?
       c. A storm?
       d. A hurricane?

7. **Where does krypton occur?**
   Is it in:

       a. An ice particle?
       b. A lightning flash?
       c. Heavy rain?
       d. The air?

8. **What is a *föhn*?**
   Is it:

       a. An Alpine summer hailstorm?
       b. A small waterspout in the South Pacific?
       c. A dry, warm wind, blowing down a mountain?
       d. A north wind, bringing snow?

9. **What kind of cloud is described as:**
   **'a large, dark cloud, often wider at its apex than at its base, which often produces thunderstorms'.**
   Is it:

       a. Cumulus?
       b. Cirrus?
       c. Cumulonimbus?
       d. Nimbostratus?

10. **Which of the following gives the correct order of the colours in the rainbow?**
    Is it:

        a. Yellow, orange, blue, green, indigo, violet, red?
        b. Green, blue, yellow, orange, red, violet, indigo?
        c. Red, orange, yellow, green, blue, indigo, violet?
        d. Violet, indigo, blue, yellow, green, orange, red?

# A MIXED BAG

1.  Victoria Crosses are made from the metal of guns
    captured from the enemy during a war. Which war?
    Was it:
    - a.  The Boer War?
    - b.  The Crimean War?
    - c.  The Zulu War?
    - d.  The First World War?

2.  Which two countries does the 49th parallel divide?
    Is it:
    - a.  China and Mongolia?
    - b.  Angola and Namibia?
    - c.  Bolivia and Argentina?
    - d.  Canada and the USA?

3.  In which game does 'sooping' take place?
    Is it in:
    - a.  Curling?
    - b.  Ice hockey?
    - c.  Croquet?
    - d.  Basketball?

4.  Where are the Maldive Islands?
    - a.  In the South Pacific Ocean?
    - b.  In the South Atlantic Ocean?
    - c.  In the northern Indian Ocean?
    - d.  In the Coral Sea?

5.  Who was the Norse god of thunder?
    Was it:
    - a.  Vulcan?
    - b.  Jupiter?
    - c.  Thor?
    - d.  Odin?

6. **What is 1,000,000,000 called in the USA?**
   Is it:
   - a. One thousand million?
   - b. One million?
   - c. One billion?
   - d. One trillion?

7. **When was the Race Against Time, the biggest ever charity fun run?**
   Was it:
   - a. 12 May 1988?
   - b. 20 August 1988?
   - c. 11 September 1988?
   - d. 15 October 1988?

8. **What are Asante, Bemba, Tuareg and Galla?**
   Are they:
   - a. Typefaces?
   - b. Grades of silk?
   - c. Blends of tea?
   - d. African languages?

9. **Who was known as the 'Louisville Lip'?**
   Was it:
   - a. Joe Louis?
   - b. Rocky Marciano?
   - c. Tommy Burns?
   - d. Muhammad Ali?

10. **What is a colchicum?**
    Is it:
    - a. An autumn crocus?
    - b. A grape hyacinth?
    - c. An anemone?
    - d. A night-scented stock?

# OLYMPIC GAMES

1. **When were the Olympic Games held in London?**
   **Was it in:**
   - a. 1932?
   - b. 1948?
   - c. 1952?
   - d. 1956?

2. **Who is the only woman to have won three gold medals for figure skating? (She also won the World Championship ten times.)**
   **Was it:**
   - a. Carol Heiss?
   - b. Sonja Henie?
   - c. Katarina Witt?
   - d. Anett Pötzsch?

3. **Which swimmer, nicknamed 'The Albatross', set Olympic records in 1984 in the 200 Metres Freestyle and the 100 Metres Butterfly?**
   **Was it:**
   - a. Steve Lundquist?
   - b. Rick Carey?
   - c. Alex Baumann?
   - d. Michael Gross?

4. **In which Olympic Games did the Princess Royal compete?**
   **Was it in:**
   - a. 1972?
   - b. 1976?
   - c. 1980?
   - d. Never?

5. In which race did Sebastian Coe set an Olympic record in 1984?
   Was it in:
   - a. The 400 metres?
   - b. The 800 metres?
   - c. The 1500 metres?
   - d. The 5000 metres?

6. Who holds the greatest number of Olympic medals?
   Is it:
   - a. Nikolai Andrianov?
   - b. Olga Korbut?
   - c. Larissa Latynina?
   - d. Lyudmila Tourischeva?

7. Mark Spitz won seven gold medals at one Olympic Games. Which one?
   Was it the:
   - a. 1972?
   - b. 1976?
   - c. 1980?
   - d. 1984?

8. In which event did Daley Thompson take the gold medal in both the 1980 and 1984 Olympics?
   Was it in the:
   - a. Javelin?
   - b. Discus?
   - c. 110 Metres Hurdles?
   - d. Decathlon?

9. Tessa Sanderson set an Olympic record in 1984. In which event?
   Was it in:
   - a. The Long Jump?
   - b. The Javelin?
   - c. The Shot?
   - d. The Discus?

10. In which event in the 1984 Olympics did Reiner Klimke win a gold medal?
    Was it in:
    - a. Dressage?
    - b. Featherweight boxing?
    - c. The Biathlon?
    - d. The 1000 Metres Canoe Race?

# A MIXED BAG

1. **Which capital city is the coldest in the world?**
   Is it:
   - a. Moscow?
   - b. Ottawa?
   - c. Ulan Bator?
   - d. Reykjavik?

2. **How many seats were sold in London's West End theatres in 1987?**
   Was it:
   - a. 400,000?
   - b. 3,000,000?
   - c. Almost 11,000,000?
   - d. More than 12,000,000?

3. **What is a mansard?**
   Is it:
   - a. A house inhabited by a Church of England minister?
   - b. A roof with each face having two slopes?
   - c. A rope railing?
   - d. A country house set in an estate?

4. **Which aeroplane was called the Flying Fortress?**
   Was it:
   - a. A Boeing B-17?
   - b. A Douglas DC-3?
   - c. A Gramman F-14?
   - d. A Sopwith Camel?

5.  **What is the difference between horns and antlers?**
    **Is it the fact that:**
    a. Horns grown on sheep, goats and cows; antlers grow on antelopes and deer?
    b. Horns are straight and antlers are curved?
    c. Horns grow on both sexes of some animals and continue to grow all their lives; antlers grow on male deer and are renewed?
    d. Horns are made of bone; antlers of a nail-like substance?

6.  **What is a portcullis?**
    **Is it:**
    a. An entrance to a port?
    b. A suspended grating which can be raised or lowered at the entrance of a castle?
    c. A portable gate, like a sheep hurdle?
    d. A large covered entrance for vehicles leading into a courtyard?

7.  **Who wrote *Fat Is a Feminist Issue*?**
    **Was it:**
    a. Germaine Greer?
    b. Marilyn French?
    c. Sarah Kennedy?
    d. Susie Orbach?

8.  **What is a chukka?**
    **Is it:**
    a. A North American partridge?
    b. A thrown object?
    c. A period of continuous play in polo?
    d. A wheel on a wooden cart?

9.  **When was the Panama Canal completed?**
    **Was it in:**
    a. 1850?
    b. 1900?
    c. 1914?
    d. 1930?

**10. What was Belize formerly called?**
**Was it:**

      a. British Honduras?
      b. British Guiana?
      c. Cameroon?
      d. El Salvador?

# NOVEL EXPERIENCE

1. **In which Dickens novel does Sam Weller appear?**
   Is it:
   - a. *David Copperfield*?
   - b. *The Pickwick Papers*?
   - c. *Our Mutual Friend*?
   - d. *The Old Curiosity Shop*?

2. **Which one of these fictional characters is *not* a detective?**
   Is it:
   - a. Father Brown?
   - b. Lord Peter Wimsey?
   - c. George Smiley?
   - d. Albert Campion?

3. **Which Jane Austen novel begins: 'It is a truth universally acknowledged, that a single man in possession of a good fortune, must be in want of a wife.'**
   Is it:
   - a. *Sense and Sensibility*?
   - b. *Persuasion*?
   - c. *Northanger Abbey*?
   - d. *Pride and Prejudice*?

4. **Who wrote *The History Man*?**
   Was it:
   - a. Malcolm Bradbury?
   - b. Kingsley Amis?
   - c. Tom Sharpe?
   - d. Wilbur Smith?

5. **What was the occupation of Diggory Venn in Thomas Hardy's novel *The Return of the Native*?**
   Was it:
   a. Shepherd?
   b. Publican?
   c. Reddleman?
   d. Furze cutter?

6. **Which one of these books is *not* by John Le Carré?**
   Is it:
   a. *The Spy Who Came in From the Cold*?
   b. *Gorky Park*?
   c. *The Naive and Sentimental Lover*?
   d. *The Honourable Schoolboy*?

7. **In which of the following books is Charles Pooter of The Laurels, Holloway, the chief character?**
   Is it:
   a. *Diary of a Nobody*?
   b. *Barchester Towers*?
   c. *Erewhon*?
   d. *Clayhanger*?

8. **Which one of these thriller writers is a former jockey, famous for an incident involving the Queen Mother's horse?**
   Is it:
   a. Jeffrey Archer?
   b. Hammond Innes?
   c. John Francombe?
   d. Dick Francis?

9. **What was the name of Lord Emsworth's pig in the P.G. Wodehouse books?**
   Was it:
   a. Eustacia?
   b. Empress of Blandings?
   c. Lady Serena Emsworth?
   d. The Duchess of Emsworth?

10. The play, *The Fifteen Streets*, is based on a book by one of Britain's best-selling novelists. Which of the following authors wrote it?
    Was it:
    a. Barbara Cartland?
    b. Barbara Taylor Bradford?
    c. Catherine Cookson?
    d. Sally Beauman?

# A MIXED BAG

1. **Who was the world's first four-minute miler?**
   **Was it:**
   - a. Emil Zatopek?
   - b. Chris Chataway?
   - c. Chris Brasher?
   - d. Roger Bannister?

2. **What does rebarbative mean?**
   **Is it:**
   - a. Repellent and unattractive?
   - b. Sharp in retort?
   - c. Astringent?
   - d. Sleep-inducing?

3. **When was the first Crusade?**
   **Was it in:**
   - a. 985?
   - b. 1015?
   - c. 1095?
   - d. 1245?

4. **Who wrote a humorous piece of music called the Coffee Cantata?**
   **Was it:**
   - a. Bach?
   - b. Benjamin Britten?
   - c. Arthur Sullivan?
   - d. Cole Porter?

5. **What is a chantry?**
   **Is it:**
   - a. A priest privately employed by a rich family?
   - b. A specially endowed chapel?
   - c. A male sheep under two years old?
   - d. A young male chicken?

6. **When did the last tram run in London?**
   Was it:
   - a. 1948?
   - b. 1952?
   - c. 1958?
   - d. 1962?

7. **What is a cwm?**
   Is it:
   - a. A baby's cot?
   - b. A badger's nest?
   - c. A river bed?
   - d. A rounded hollow in a mountainside?

8. **What is or was the Maquis?**
   Is/was it:
   - a. A desert?
   - b. The French Resistance in the Second World War?
   - c. A French nobleman?
   - d. A French gold coin?

9. **What connects Neil Armstrong, Alan Shepard and Eugene Cernan?**
   Is it that:
   - a. They have all climbed Mount Everest without breathing equipment?
   - b. They were all aides of Ronald Reagan at the White House?
   - c. They have all sailed round the world single-handed?
   - d. They have all walked on the moon?

10. **What is gumbo?**
    Is it:
    - a. A preparation for cleaning walking boots, etc.?
    - b. Soil which turns to sticky mud in the rain?
    - c. A paste for cleaning iron stoves?
    - d. The material from which boxers' gumshields are made?

# THE RULING CLASS

1. **Whose wife was called the 'fair maid of Kent'?**
   Was it:
   - a. Richard I?
   - b. Richard II?
   - c. Edward, the Black Prince?
   - d. Edward III?

2. **Who lives at Kensington Palace?**
   Is it:
   - a. Prince and Princess Michael of Kent?
   - b. The Prince and Princess of Wales?
   - c. Princess Margaret?
   - d. All of the above?

3. **Where was Queen Elizabeth II born?**
   Was it at:
   - a. Windsor Castle?
   - b. Buckingham Palace?
   - c. St Thomas's Hospital?
   - d. Bruton Street, London?

4. **To whom was Queen Elizabeth I married?**
   Was it:
   - a. The Earl of Essex?
   - b. The Earl of Leicester?
   - c. King Philip II of Spain?
   - d. No one?

5. **Which member of the Royal Family was born Birgitte Eva van Deurs?**
   Is it:
   - a. The Duchess of Kent?
   - b. The Duchess of Gloucester?
   - c. Princess Michael of Kent?
   - d. The Duchess of Westminster?

6. **When was Princess Margaret's marriage to Lord Snowdon dissolved?**
   Was it in:
   - a. 1977?
   - b. 1978?
   - c. 1979?
   - d. 1980?

7. **When was Edward VIII king of England?**
   Was it:
   - a. Never?
   - b. 20 January to 11 December 1936?
   - c. 1 January to 10 December 1937?
   - d. 31 January to 10 October 1936?

8. **Which member of the Royal Family runs an interior decorating business?**
   Is it:
   - a. Viscount Linley?
   - b. Marina Ogilvy?
   - c. Lady Sarah Armstrong-Jones?
   - d. Princess Michael of Kent?

9. **Whose children are George Philip Nicholas, Earl of St Andrews; Lady Helen Windsor; and Lord Nicholas Windsor?**
   Are they the children of:
   - a. The Duke and Duchess of Kent?
   - b. Prince and Princess Michael of Kent?
   - c. Princess Alexandra and the Hon. Angus Ogilvy?
   - d. The Princess Royal and Captain Mark Phillips?

10. **Who is fourth in the Order of Succession to the Crown?**
    Is it:
    - a. Prince Henry?
    - b. The Princess Royal?
    - c. Prince Andrew?
    - d. Prince Edward?

# A MIXED BAG

1. **Which towns were the original Cinque Ports?**
   Were they:
   - a. Winchelsea, Hastings, Dover, Rye, Romney?
   - b. Hastings, Sandwich, Dover, Romney, Rye?
   - c. Hastings, Pevensey, Winchelsea, Dover, Rye?
   - d. Appledore, Hastings, Sandwich, Dover, Hythe?

2. **Who was Elizabeth I's mother?**
   Was it:
   - a. Eleanor of Aquitaine?
   - b. Catherine Howard?
   - c. Anne Boleyn?
   - d. Catherine of Aragon?

3. **At which spot do cross-channel swimmers land in Britain?**
   Is it:
   - a. Dover?
   - b. St Margaret's Bay?
   - c. Deal?
   - d. Kingsdown?

4. **To which group of fish does a lemon sole belong?**
   Is it:
   - a. Sole?
   - b. Plaice?
   - c. Haddock?
   - d. Bream?

5. **How many martello towers were built along the south coast as a defence against Napoleon?**
   Was it:
   - a. Fifty?
   - b. Seventy-four?
   - c. Thirty-two?
   - d. Nine?

6. Which town did Jane Austen use as a background for *Mansfield Park*?
   Was it:
   - a. Hothfield?
   - b. Lympne?
   - c. Wye?
   - d. Godmersham?

7. Who discovered how blood circulates?
   Was it:
   - a. Sir Isaac Newton?
   - b. John Napier?
   - c. William Harvey?
   - d. William Herbert?

8. Which year did the Dartford Tunnel open?
   Was it:
   - a. 1971?
   - b. 1955?
   - c. 1963?
   - d. 1968?

9. Where did Dickens write *David Copperfield*, a place which now holds a Dickens Festival?
   Was it:
   - a. Eastchurch?
   - b. Lynsted?
   - c. Broadstairs?
   - d. Margate?

10. Where is King Harold believed to have been buried after the Battle of Hastings?
    Was it:
    - a. Waltham Abbey?
    - b. St Albans?
    - c. Glastonbury?
    - d. Windsor Castle?

# SCIENTISTS AND INVENTORS

1.  **Which mathematician was known as the father of computing?**
    Was it:
    - a. Euclid?
    - b. Charles Babbage?
    - c. George Boole?
    - d. Robert Noyce?

2.  **Which American statesman invented the lightning conductor?**
    Was it:
    - a. Benjamin Franklin?
    - b. George Washington?
    - c. Theodore Roosevelt?
    - d. Abraham Lincoln?

3.  **For which theory did Albert Einstein receive the Nobel Prize for Physics?**
    Was it:
    - a. The theory of relativity?
    - b. The quantum theory?
    - c. The photoelectric effect?
    - d. The electromagnetic theory?

4.  **Who invented the ballpoint pen?**
    Was it:
    - a. Georg and Laszlo Biro?
    - b. Henri Bic?
    - c. Lewis Waterman?
    - d. Peter Parker?

5. In 1850 James Harrison of Britain and Alexander Catlin Twining of the USA invented a useful piece of household equipment.
   Was it:
     a. The vacuum cleaner?
     b. The electric kettle?
     c. The refrigerator?
     d. The electric cooker?

6. Which one of these physicists discovered radioactivity?
   Was it:
     a. Wilhelm Röntgen?
     b. Pierre Curie?
     c. John Cockcroft?
     d. Antoine Becquerel?

7. Who was the first man to believe that the Earth went round the Sun, rather than the other way around?
   Was it:
     a. Archimedes?
     b. Nicholaus Copernicus?
     c. Leonardo da Vinci?
     d. Galileo Galilei?

8. Alfred Bernhard Nobel, who left his fortune to endow the Nobel Prizes, was a chemist and inventor. What did he invent?
   Was it:
     a. Dynamite?
     b. Penicillin?
     c. The gramophone?
     d. The vacuum flask?

9. In which group of islands did Charles Darwin make his observations about the evolution of species?
   Was it in:
     a. The Seychelles?
     b. The Azores?
     c. The New Hebrides?
     d. The Galapagos?

10. **Who established the laws of heredity?**
    Was it:
    a. Linnaeus?
    b. Gregor Mendel?
    c. Francis Crick?
    d. James Young Simpson?

# A MIXED BAG

1. **Who was the first man to swim 100 metres in less than a minute and became a Hollywood star?**
   **Was it:**
   - a. Clark Gable?
   - b. Gregory Peck?
   - c. Stewart Granger?
   - d. Johnny Weismuller?

2. **What are the Royal Navy's Sharks?**
   **Are they:**
   - a. Submarines?
   - b. Underwater missiles?
   - c. Sea to air missiles?
   - d. A team of display helicopters?

3. **Who won the 1988 St Leger?**
   **Was it:**
   - a. Diminuendo?
   - b. Sheriff's Star?
   - c. Minster Son?
   - d. Zaffaran?

4. **What does the carat of a diamond measure?**
   **Is it its:**
   - a. Size?
   - b. Weight?
   - c. Colour?
   - d. Clarity?

5. **Which explorer discovered the route to India round the Cape of Good Hope?**
   **Was it:**
   - a. Vasco da Gama?
   - b. Ferdinand Magellan?
   - c. Christopher Columbus?
   - d. Marco Polo?

6. **What is the average daily temperature in England?**
Is it:
   - a. 9.8°C?
   - b. 10.1°C?
   - c. 11.5°C?
   - d. 12°C?

7. **When was the hurricane that devastated southern England?**
Was it:
   - a. 18–19 October 1986?
   - b. 12–13 March 1987?
   - c. 15–16 October 1987?
   - d. 31 October–1 November 1987?

8. **Whose motto is *Per ardua ad astra*?**
Is it:
   - a. British Airways'?
   - b. The RAF's?
   - c. Rolls Royce's?
   - d. The Prince of Wales's?

9. **Who sold Alaska to the USA?**
Was it:
   - a. Canada?
   - b. Great Britain?
   - c. Denmark?
   - d. Russia?

10. **Who won the Panasonic European Open Golf Championship in 1988?**
Was it:
   - a. Nick Faldo?
   - b. Denis Durnian?
   - c. Ian Woosnam?
   - d. Sandy Lyle?

# CARS OVER THE YEARS

1. **In which year did the Mini first appear?**
   **Was it in:**
   - a. 1958?
   - b. 1959?
   - c. 1960?
   - d. 1961?

2. **Which manufacturers produced cars called Oxford and Cambridge?**
   **Was it:**
   - a. Jaguar and Triumph?
   - b. Bentley and Daimler?
   - c. Morris and Austin?
   - d. Sunbeam and Ford?

3. **Who made a car called the Grey Lady?**
   **Was it:**
   - a. Rolls Royce?
   - b. Alvis?
   - c. Armstrong-Siddeley?
   - d. Lea Francis?

4. **When did a Mustang chase a Charger round the streets of San Francisco?**
   **Was it in the film:**
   - a. *Bullitt*?
   - b. *The Love Bug*?
   - c. *The Yellow Rolls Royce*?
   - d. *The Spy Who Loved Me*?

5. **For how long was the Volkswagen Beetle produced?**
   **Was it for:**
   - a. Twenty years?
   - b. Thirty years?
   - c. Thirty-nine years?
   - d. Forty-four years?

6. **Each of these silhouettes represents a decade of car design.**
   **Which is which?**
      a. 1930s.
      b. 1950s.
      c. 1960s.
      d. 1980s.

7. **Which car manufacturer depicts a rearing black horse as its badge?**
   **Is it:**
      a. BMW?
      b. Lamborghini?
      c. Ferrari?
      d. Porsche?

8. **What connects the Bond Bug, the 1927 Morgan, the Reliant Robin and the BSA Scout?**
   **Is it that:**
      a. They were all made in Tamworth?
      b. They were all produced in only two colours – red and black?
      c. They were all produced before 1930?
      d. They were all three-wheelers?

9. **Which of the terms below is described by 'A car with a drophead body, large enough to carry four people in comfort. In the past it may have had a division between driver and passengers.'**
   **Is it:**
      a. A saloon?
      b. A coupé?
      c. A cabriolet?
      d. A sedanca de ville?

10. **Which one of the following luxury car manufacturers is *not* owned by a large conglomerate?**

Is it:

   a. Aston Martin?
   b. Jaguar?
   c. Maserati?
   d. Ferrari?

# A MIXED BAG

1. **What is chamber music?**
   **Is it:**
       a. Music for a string quartet?
       b. Music performed without a conductor?
       c. Music intended to be played in a small room, with few performers?
       d. Music intended to be played in churches?

2. **Approximately how many people were killed in the Second World War?**
   **Was it:**
       a. 20.75 million?
       b. 38.7 million?
       c. 54.8 million?
       d. 85.4 million?

3. **Who or what is a John Dory?**
   **Is he or it:**
       a. A fish?
       b. An MP elected on the slenderest of majorities?
       c. A style of house-building?
       d. A sea shanty?

4. **What is the flying distance between London and Hong Kong?**
   **Is it:**
       a. 7585 kilometres?
       b. 8765 kilometres?
       c. 9640 kilometres?
       d. 10,470 kilometres?

5. **What have Normandy, Blois, Anjou and Grey in common?**
   Is it that:
   - a. They are all wine-growing regions of France?
   - b. They were all royal houses of England?
   - c. They are all parts of France that have been owned by England?
   - d. They are all towns in Mississippi, USA?

6. **When was the Battle of Bosworth Field fought?**
   Was it:
   - a. In 1455?
   - b. In 1485?
   - c. In 1492?
   - d. In 1517?

7. **What latitude is the Tropic of Cancer?**
   Is it:
   - a. 23°N?
   - b. 23°S?
   - c. 30°N?
   - d. 30°S?

8. **What colour is the stone called a cairngorm?**
   Is it:
   - a. Black?
   - b. Greenish-blue?
   - c. Pinkish-brown?
   - d. Smoky yellow or brown?

9. **What do the letters WHO stand for?**
   Is it:
   - a. The *Worcester and Hereford Observer*?
   - b. Women's Health Officer?
   - c. West Hebridean Ocean?
   - d. World Health Organisation?

10. **When was Milton Keynes built?**
    Was it in:
    - a. 1961?
    - b. 1967?
    - c. 1970?
    - d. 1973?

# ON THE BOX

1. **Who played the elderly lady detective in the *Miss Marple* series?**
   Was it:
   a. Joan Hickson?
   b. Thora Hird?
   c. Patricia Hayes?
   d. Peggy Ashcroft?

2. **On which TV channel are the Proms televised?**
   Is it:
   a. BBC 1?
   b. BBC 2?
   c. ITV?
   d. Channel 4?

3. **How are William Tarmey and Elizabeth Dawn better known?**
   Is it as:
   a. Ken and Deirdre Barlow in *Coronation Street*?
   b. Jack and Vera Duckworth in *Coronation Street*?
   c. Wicksy and Michelle in *EastEnders*?
   d. Alison and Harry in *Brookside*?

4. **In which TV regular does Barnsdale appear?**
   Is it in:
   a. *Dr Kildare*?
   b. *Emmerdale Farm*?
   c. *In Sickness and in Health*?
   d. *Gardeners' World*?

5. **What connects *The Sullivans* and *Neighbours*?**
   Is it that:
   a. They have the same star?
   b. They are both set in America?
   c. They are both set in Australia?
   d. They are both on ITV?

6. What was the occupation of Lovejoy in the series of that name?
   Was he:
   - a. A policeman?
   - b. An antiques dealer?
   - c. An artist?
   - d. A courier?

7. Who are Tyne Daly and Sharon Gless better known as?
   Is it:
   - a. The Krankies?
   - b. Inspector Kate Longton and Sergeant Beck?
   - c. Cagney and Lacey?
   - d. French and Saunders?

8. Which series features Hawkeye, B.J. and Hotlips?
   Is it:
   - a. *M.A.S.H.*?
   - b. *The New Avengers*?
   - c. *Bewitched*?
   - d. *'Allo 'Allo!*?

9. Who says *Good Morning Britain*?
   Is it:
   - a. John Stapleton and Sally James?
   - b. Jeremy Paxman and Kirsty Wark?
   - c. Kay Burley and Mike Morris?
   - d. Mike Morris and Kathy Taylor?

10. Who goes *In at the Deep End*?
    Is it:
    - a. Roy Castle and Cheryl Baker?
    - b. Chris Serle and Paul Heiney?
    - c. Alan Titchmarsh and Pamela Armstrong?
    - d. Martyn Lewis and Andrew Harvey?

## A MIXED BAG

1. **In what year was the late John Betjeman appointed Poet Laureate?**
   Was it:
   - a. 1950?
   - b. 1972?
   - c. 1969?
   - d. 1975?

2. **Which wife of Henry VIII was Catherine Howard?**
   Was she:
   - a. First?
   - b. Fourth?
   - c. Second?
   - d. Fifth?

3. **What is another name for the Russian Revolution?**
   Is it:
   - a. The Peasants' Revolt?
   - b. The Year of Martyrs?
   - c. The February Revolution?
   - d. The March Revolution?

4. **Which one of the following is a private home of the Queen?**
   - a. Windsor Castle?
   - b. Hampton Court Palace?
   - c. Balmoral Castle?
   - d. The Palace of Holyroodhouse?

5. **Which mountain in the United States has the faces of several presidents carved into its side?**
   Is it:
   - a. Mount St Helens?
   - b. Mount Palomar?
   - c. Mount Kennedy?
   - d. Mount Rushmore?

6. **What is a panama hat made of?**
   **Is it:**
   - a. Felt?
   - b. Leather?
   - c. Plaited leaves?
   - d. Bamboo?

7. **What is one function of the pancreas gland?**
   **Does it:**
   - a. Detoxify poisons?
   - b. Secrete bile?
   - c. Control growth?
   - d. Secrete insulin?

8. **Which one of these colours is *not* a primary colour?**
   **Is it:**
   - a. Red?
   - b. Black?
   - c. Blue?
   - d. Yellow?

9. **What comprises the Cross of Lorraine?**
   **Does it have:**
   - a. Two horizontal bars above and below the midpoint of the vertical bar, the lower longer than the upper?
   - b. Vertical and horizontal bars which cross at midpoint?
   - c. Bars similar to what is now called a swastika?
   - d. A fleur-de-lis at both ends of each bar?

10. **What is Benelux?**
    **Is it:**
    - a. A soap powder?
    - b. An organisation promoting tourism in Belgium, the Netherlands and Luxembourg?
    - c. An airline owned by the above countries?
    - d. A customs and economics union of the above countries?

# MAKING DATES

1. **When was Aristotle alive?**
   **Was it in:**
   - a. The first century AD?
   - b. The first century BC?
   - c. The third century BC?
   - d. The fourth century BC?

2. **When was the first decimal coin circulated in Britain?**
   **Was it in:**
   - a. 1968?
   - b. 1969?
   - c. 1970?
   - d. 1971?

3. **When was the Battle of Waterloo?**
   **Was it in:**
   - a. 1812?
   - b. 1815?
   - c. 1820?
   - d. 1823?

4. **When did Macbeth murder Duncan of Scotland?**
   **Was it in:**
   - a. 1020?
   - b. 1040?
   - c. 1080?
   - d. 1120?

5. **When did the Boer War start?**
   **Was it in:**
   - a. 1888?
   - b. 1889?
   - c. 1898?
   - d. 1899?

6. **When was the Battle of Agincourt?**
   Was it in:
   - a. 1066?
   - b. 1215?
   - c. 1415?
   - d. 1450?

7. **When did Queen Victoria die?**
   Was it in:
   - a. 1895?
   - b. 1898?
   - c. 1900?
   - d. 1901?

8. **When was the Peasants' Revolt?**
   Was it in:
   - a. 1292?
   - b. 1300?
   - c. 1381?
   - d. 1434?

9. **When was the Beeching Report published, resulting in large-scale closure of Britain's railways?**
   Was it in:
   - a. 1960?
   - b. 1963?
   - c. 1965?
   - d. 1968?

10. **When was Thomas a Becket murdered in Canterbury Cathedral?**
    Was it in:
    - a. 1170?
    - b. 1190?
    - c. 1250?
    - d. 1290?

# A MIXED BAG

1. **Who lives at 11 Downing Street?**
   Is it:
   - a. The Home Secretary?
   - b. The Foreign Secretary?
   - c. The Chancellor of the Exchequer?
   - d. The Leader of the Opposition?

2. **In which of these countries was Sanskrit the ancient language?**
   Was it in:
   - a. Egypt?
   - b. India?
   - c. China?
   - d. Iran?

3. **What are an individual's chances of being killed by lightning?**
   Are they:
   - a. One in 100,000?
   - b. One in 1,000,000?
   - c. One in 5,000,000?
   - d. One in 50,000,000?

4. **Which of the heroes of *The Three Musketeers* was not a musketeer at the start of the book?**
   Was it:
   - a. Aramis?
   - b. Athos?
   - c. Porthos?
   - d. D'Artagnan?

5. **Which country does the rugby team the Chanticleers come from?**
Is it:
   - a. France?
   - b. Britain?
   - c. New Zealand?
   - d. South Africa?

6. **Which of the current BBC radio stations used to be called the Home Service?**
Is it:
   - a. Radio 1?
   - b. Radio 2?
   - c. Radio 3?
   - d. Radio 4?

7. **If it is 3 pm in London, what time is it in New York?**
Is it:
   - a. 9 am?
   - b. 10 am?
   - c. 9 pm?
   - d. 12 noon?

8. **What was the city of Beijing formerly known as?**
Was it:
   - a. Shanghai?
   - b. Hanoi?
   - c. Phnom Penh?
   - d. Peking?

9. **When did Virginia Wade win the Women's Singles Championship at Wimbledon?**
Was it:
   - a. In 1977?
   - b. In 1979?
   - c. In 1981?
   - d. Never?

10. **What does *festina lente* mean?**
Is it:
   - a. Highly decorated?
   - b. Keep to the left?
   - c. Left to rot?
   - d. To hurry slowly?

# THE WORKS OF THE BARD

1. **Who was Prospero's daughter?**
   **Was she:**
   - a. Miranda?
   - b. Ariel?
   - c. Rosalind?
   - d. Portia?

2. **Who said, 'Friends, Romans, countrymen, lend me your ears . . .'?**
   **Was it:**
   - a. Brutus?
   - b. Cassius?
   - c. Casca?
   - d. Mark Antony?

3. **In which play do Sir Andrew Aguecheek and Sir Toby Belch appear?**
   **Is it:**
   - a. *As You Like It*?
   - b. *The Merry Wives of Windsor*?
   - c. *Twelfth Night*?
   - d. *The Winter's Tale*?

4. **Who chose the right casket and won the lady in *The Merchant of Venice*?**
   **Was it:**
   - a. Antonio?
   - b. Bassanio?
   - c. The Prince of Morocco?
   - d. The Prince of Arragon?

5. **Whom did Friar Lawrence marry?**
   **Was it:**
   - a. Romeo and Juliet?
   - b. Jessica and Lorenzo?
   - c. Rosalind and Orlando?
   - d. Olivia and Sebastian?

6. **In which play is an entire scene written in French?**
   Is it in:
   - a. *Richard II*?
   - b. *Henry IV Part II*?
   - c. *Henry V*?
   - d. *Cymbeline*?

7. **Who were the two gentlemen of Verona?**
   Were they:
   - a. Ferdinand and Antonio?
   - b. Claudio and Benedick?
   - c. Rosencrantz and Guildenstern?
   - d. Valentine and Proteus?

8. **Who killed Macbeth?**
   Was it:
   - a. Lady Macbeth?
   - b. Macduff?
   - c. Malcolm?
   - d. Young Siward?

9. **Whose downfall was brought about by a handkerchief?**
   Was it:
   - a. Desdemona's?
   - b. Lady Macbeth's?
   - c. Cleopatra's?
   - d. Hamlet's?

10. **Who cried, 'A horse! a horse! my kingdom for a horse!'?**
    Was it:
    - a. Richard II?
    - b. Richard III?
    - c. Henry V?
    - d. Hamlet?

# A MIXED BAG

1.  **Where is Mount Elizabeth?**
    **Is it in:**
    - a. Kenya?
    - b. South Africa?
    - c. Canada?
    - d. Antarctica?

2.  **Which way does the tail of a comet point?**
    **Is it:**
    - a. Towards the Sun?
    - b. Away from the Sun?
    - c. Towards the Earth?
    - d. Away from the Earth?

3.  **What does a becquerel measure?**
    **Is it:**
    - a. Radiation activity?
    - b. Illumination?
    - c. Latent heat?
    - d. Inductance?

4.  **Who wrote *Murder in the Cathedral*?**
    **Was it:**
    - a. Dorothy Sayers?
    - b. W.H. Auden?
    - c. T.S. Eliot?
    - d. Agatha Christie?

5.  **When is the Queen's official birthday?**
    **Is it:**
    - a. 21 April?
    - b. 31 May?
    - c. 2 June?
    - d. The second Saturday in June?

6. **Which US state is known as the 'Heart of Dixie'?**
   Is it:
   - a. Alabama?
   - b. Louisiana?
   - c. Georgia?
   - d. Mississippi?

7. **When was the Boy Scout movement founded?**
   Was it in:
   - a. 1901?
   - b. 1903?
   - c. 1907?
   - d. 1925?

8. **When the time in London is twelve noon, what time is it in Singapore?**
   Is it:
   - a. 9 am?
   - b. 3 pm?
   - c. 7.30 pm?
   - d. 9 pm?

9. **What unit is used to measure electric current?**
   Is it:
   - a. The ampère?
   - b. The volt?
   - c. The ohm?
   - d. The watt?

10. **When did the English Civil War begin?**
    Was it in:
    - a. 1642?
    - b. 1644?
    - c. 1646?
    - d. 1648?

# FUNNY HA HA

1. **Who played Bluebottle in *The Goon Show*?**
   **Was it:**
   - a. Harry Secombe?
   - b. Michael Bentine?
   - c. Spike Milligan?
   - d. Peter Sellers?

2. **Which comedian is/was famous for his tickling stick?**
   **Is/was it:**
   - a. Tommy Cooper?
   - b. Ken Dodd?
   - c. Harry Worth?
   - d. Jimmy Edwards?

3. **Who did the famous impersonation of Harold Macmillan in *Beyond the Fringe*?**
   **Was it:**
   - a. Peter Cook?
   - b. Dudley Moore?
   - c. Alan Bennett?
   - d. Jonathan Miller?

4. **Which great comic star appeared in the films *The Happiest Days of Your Life* and *The Belles of St Trinian's*?**
   **Was it:**
   - a. Peter Sellers?
   - b. Ian Carmichael?
   - c. Stanley Holloway?
   - d. Alastair Sim?

5. Which of the following said: 'I hate housework! You make the beds, you do the dishes – and six months later you have to start all over again!'?
Was it:
   a. Victoria Wood?
   b. Joan Rivers?
   c. Maureen Lipman?
   d. Dame Edna Everage?

6. Who lived at 23 Railway Cuttings, East Cheam?
Was it:
   a. Anthony Aloysius Hancock?
   b. Dud and Pete?
   c. Alf Garnett and family?
   d. Mr and Mrs Glum?

7. What was the name of Steptoe and Son's horse?
Was it called:
   a. Harold?
   b. Hercules?
   c. Invincible?
   d. Bess?

8. Who, in 1976, made a comic silent film?
Was it:
   a. Woody Allen?
   b. Mel Brooks?
   c. The Boulting Brothers?
   d. Bryan Forbes?

9. In which TV comedy programme were the 'Spam Song' and the 'Lumberjack Song'?
Were they in:
   a. *Spitting Image*?
   b. *Monty Python's Flying Circus*?
   c. *Rutland Weekend Television*?
   d. *Fawlty Towers*?

10. To which long-suffering lady did Groucho Marx make such remarks as: 'You can leave in a taxi. If you can't get a taxi you can leave in a huff. If that's too soon you can leave in a minute and a huff.'?
Was it:
   a. Loretta Young?
   b. Eleanor Parker?
   c. Margaret Dumont?
   d. Ida Lupino?

# A MIXED BAG

1. **What is fuller's earth?**
   **Is it:**
   a. Sawdust from fuller's mills?
   b. A naturally absorbent clay?
   c. A type of decaying matter?
   d. A loam that absorbs odours?

2. **How many babies were born by caesarian section in England and Wales in 1987?**
   **Was it:**
   a. Nearly one in seven?
   b. Three in ten?
   c. One in a hundred?
   d. Over two in five?

3. **Which song is Canada's national anthem?**
   **Is it:**
   a. 'God Save the Queen'?
   b. 'The Maple Leaf Forever'?
   c. 'O Canada'?
   d. 'The Battle Hymn of the Republic'?

4. **What is a baby beaver called?**
   **Is it:**
   a. A cub?
   b. A pup?
   c. A kit?
   d. A kitten?

5. **In which London theatre was *Peter Pan* first produced?**
   **Was it:**
   a. The London Palladium?
   b. The Lyric?
   c. The Duke of York's?
   d. The Open Air Theatre?

6. **What is palm wine?**
   **Is it:**
   - a. The wine used on Palm Sunday in the Church of England?
   - b. A wine made of exotic fruits?
   - c. Fermented palm tree sap?
   - d. A colourless glycerin?

7. **Which of these countries does *not* use metric?**
   **Is it:**
   - a. Canada?
   - b. The USA?
   - c. Australia?
   - d. Germany?

8. **What is anthotaxy?**
   **Is it:**
   - a. A herbicide?
   - b. A method of drying and preserving flowers?
   - c. Vermin extermination?
   - d. A disease that kills cattle?

9. **Which satellite relayed the world's first live transatlantic television pictures?**
   **Was it:**
   - a. Sputnik?
   - b. Anik B?
   - c. Telstar 2?
   - d. Relay II?

10. **What is a *caveat*?**
    **Is it:**
    - a. A small cave?
    - b. A legal notice?
    - c. A gourd?
    - d. A necktie?

# RECORD BREAKERS

1. **What is the largest living thing on earth?**
   **Is it:**
   - a. A blue whale?
   - b. A giant sequoia tree?
   - c. An African bush elephant?
   - d. A South Pacific tree fern?

2. **What is the greatest authenticated age a human being has ever reached?**
   **Is it:**
   - a. 115 years 3 months?
   - b. 118 years 6 months?
   - c. 120 years 8 months?
   - d. 125 years 4 months?

3. **What is the tallest office building in the world?**
   **Is it:**
   - a. The World Trade Center, New York?
   - b. The National Westminster Bank, City of London?
   - c. The Empire State Building, New York?
   - d. The Sears Tower, Chicago?

4. **Approximately how many seats are there in the largest cinema in Great Britain?**
   **Are there:**
   - a. 2000?
   - b. 2500?
   - c. 3000?
   - d. 3500?

5. **Which is the only seaside town in Britain to have three piers?**
   Is it:
     a. Brighton?
     b. Blackpool?
     c. Southend?
     d. Skegness?

6. **How tall was the tallest human being of all time?**
   Was he:
     a. 6 ft 10 ins?
     b. 7 ft 6 ins?
     c. 8 ft 3 ins?
     d. 8 ft 11 ins?

7. **How wide is the widest street in the world?**
   Is it:
     a. 100 metres (109 yards)?
     b. 150 metres (164 yards)?
     c. 200 metres (219 yards)?
     d. 250 metres (273 yards)?

8. **What is the oldest stone-built castle in Great Britain?**
   Is it:
     a. Richmond Castle, Yorkshire?
     b. Windsor Castle?
     c. Warwick Castle?
     d. Dover Castle?

9. **Where is Europe's largest public reference library?**
   Is it in:
     a. London?
     b. Paris?
     c. Stockholm?
     d. Glasgow?

10. **How fast, according to the records, is the fastest horse in the world?**
    Is it:
      a. 37.7 mph (60.7 km/h)?
      b. 43.2 mph (69.6 km/h)?
      c. 44.9 mph (71 km/h)?
      d. 46.6 mph (75 km/h)?

# A MIXED BAG

1. **When was the Hittite civilisation?**
   **Was it approximately:**
   - a. 3400 BC to 2000 BC?
   - b. 2000 BC to 1200 BC?
   - c. 1000 BC to 500 AD?
   - d. AD 500 to AD 1500?

2. **What is a 'dolly' in cricketing terms?**
   **Is it:**
   - a. An easy hit?
   - b. An easy catch?
   - c. A score of nought?
   - d. A ball which passes near the batsman's head?

3. **Who went to Greyfriars School?**
   **Was it:**
   - a. Oliver Twist?
   - b. Greyfriars Bobby?
   - c. Billy Bunter?
   - d. Prince Charles?

4. **What is the capital of Bermuda?**
   **Is it:**
   - a. Hamilton?
   - b. Havana?
   - c. Kingston?
   - d. Port-au-Prince?

5. **When did the Queen get married?**
   **Was it in:**
   - a. 1945?
   - b. 1946?
   - c. 1947?
   - d. 1948?

6. **Which country's national airline is called Sabena?**
   Is it:
   - a. Holland?
   - b. Belgium?
   - c. Ireland?
   - d. South Africa?

7. **What is an adze?**
   Is it:
   - a. A printing block?
   - b. A South American tree?
   - c. Part of a sewing machine?
   - d. A carpenter's tool?

8. **Who sits on the Woolsack?**
   Is it:
   - a. The Prime Minister?
   - b. The Speaker of the House of Commons?
   - c. The Queen, at the State Opening of Parliament?
   - d. The Lord Chancellor?

9. **How many players are there in a polo team (not including substitutes)?**
   - a. Four?
   - b. Six?
   - c. Eight?
   - d. Twelve?

10. **What was the former name of Ethiopia?**
    Was it called:
    - s. Mesopotamia?
    - b. Macedonia?
    - c. The Gold Coast?
    - d. Abyssinia?

# CRIME AND CRIMINALS

1. **How many women did Jack the Ripper kill?**
   **Was it:**
   - a. Five?
   - b. Seven?
   - c. Eight?
   - d. Ten?

2. **Ruth Ellis was the last woman to hang in Britain. When was she hanged?**
   **Was it in:**
   - a. 1948?
   - b. 1950?
   - c. 1955?
   - d. 1959?

3. **Why did Bruce Reynolds become famous in 1963?**
   **Was he:**
   - a. A Russian spy?
   - b. A US spy caught in Russia?
   - c. A murderer convicted in a lurid case?
   - d. The brains behind the Great Train Robbery?

4. **What was Al Capone's nickname?**
   **Was it:**
   - a. Bugsy?
   - b. Scarface?
   - c. Joe Bananas?
   - d. The Terrible?

5. **Who lived at 10 Rillington Place?**
   **Was it:**
   - a. Dr Crippen?
   - b. Jack the Ripper?
   - c. John Christie?
   - d. James Hanratty?

6. **In both 1925 and 1927 a con man called Victor Lustig pulled off an amazing stunt. What was it?**
   **Did he:**
   - a. Sell the Eiffel Tower?
   - b. Sell the Statue of Liberty?
   - c. Sell London Bridge?
   - d. Sell the liner *Queen Mary*?

7. **Who was Maria Marten?**
   **Was she:**
   - a. The victim in the Red Barn murder in 1827?
   - b. A famous First World War spy?
   - c. A woman convicted of murdering her husband in 1965?
   - d. A woman believed to have been murdered by MI5 in the 1950s?

8. **What were the Kray twins' first names?**
   **Were they:**
   - a. Reginald and Ronald?
   - b. Jack and George?
   - c. Bernard and Bertie?
   - d. Charles and Harold?

9. **What was the name of the criminal known as the 'Birdman of Alcatraz'?**
   **Was it:**
   - a. Benjamin Siegel?
   - b. Albert de Salvo?
   - c. Charles Starkweather?
   - d. Robert Franklin Stroud?

10. **'The Texas Rattlesnake' and 'Suicide Sal' were better known as who?**
    **Were they:**
    - a. Bonnie and Clyde?
    - b. The Dalton Gang?
    - c. Machine-gun Kelly and Belle Starr?
    - d. The Wild Bunch?

# A MIXED BAG

1. **Who was the last monarch to rule over Scotland alone?**
   Was it:
   - a. Mary, Queen of Scots?
   - b. James VI?
   - c. Robert III?
   - d. Malcolm IV?

2. **When was the United Nations set up?**
   Was it:
   - a. 1918?
   - b. 1945?
   - c. 1948?
   - d. 1950?

3. **Why was the fish used in early Christian times as a symbol of Christ?**
   Was it because:
   - a. The Greek word for 'fish' was composed of the initial letters of the words meaning Jesus Christ, Son of God, Saviour?
   - b. Of the miracle of the loaves and the fishes?
   - c. A number of the disciples were fishermen?
   - d. Christ and the disciples ate no meat?

4. **Which Greek philosopher lived in a barrel?**
   Was it:
   - a. Aristotle?
   - b. Plato?
   - c. Epicurus?
   - d. Diogenes?

5. **Which big London theatre is famous for its spectacular stage shows, concerts by international stars, and Sunday night TV entertainment?**
   Is it the:
   - a. Piccadilly?
   - b. Apollo?
   - c. Palladium?
   - d. Victoria Palace?

6. **What does a hertz measure?**
   Is it:
   - a. Frequency?
   - b. Force?
   - c. Power?
   - d. Sound?

7. **What is the birthstone for December?**
   Is it:
   - a. Garnet?
   - b. Turquoise?
   - c. Ruby?
   - d. Amethyst?

8. **What is an affluent?**
   Is it:
   - a. A rich man or woman?
   - b. A tributary stream flowing into a larger stream or river?
   - c. A conduit for a stream of waste water?
   - d. Someone who speaks a number of languages?

9. **When was Shakespeare born?**
   Was it:
   - a. 1558?
   - b. 1564?
   - c. 1580?
   - d. 1590?

10. **What is paper measuring 297 × 210 mm known as?**
    Is it:
    - a. A4?
    - b. A5?
    - c. Foolscap?
    - d. Quarto?

# MUSICAL MISCELLANY

1. **Who wrote the 1812 Overture?**
   **Was it?**
   - a. Borodin?
   - b. Mussorgsky?
   - c. Mahler?
   - d. Tchaikovsky?

2. **When was the musical *Salad Days* first produced?**
   **Was it in:**
   - a. The 1900s?
   - b. The 1920s?
   - c. The 1940s?
   - d. The 1950s?

3. **Who wrote the libretto of Kurt Weill's *The Threepenny Opera*?**
   **Was it:**
   - a. Henrik Ibsen?
   - b. Bertolt Brecht?
   - c. Johann W. von Goethe?
   - d. Hermann Hesse?

4. **Which of the following terms means that notes on bowed stringed instruments should be plucked?**
   **Is it:**
   - a. *Andante*?
   - b. *Vivace*?
   - c. *Pizzicato*?
   - d. *Con brio*?

5. **In which opera does Scarpia appear?**
   **Is it:**
   - a. *Tosca*?
   - b. *La Traviata*?
   - c. *Aida*?
   - d. *Don Giovanni*?

6. **How many strings has a violin?**
   Has it:
   - a. Three?
   - b. Four?
   - c. Six?
   - d. Eight?

7. **What is a *barcarolle*?**
   Is it:
   - a. A kind of medieval mandolin?
   - b. A term meaning with regular rhythm?
   - c. A duet for soprano and tenor?
   - d. A Venetian boating song?

8. **Who wrote the opera *Death in Venice*?**
   Was it:
   - a. Michael Tippett?
   - b. Benjamin Britten?
   - c. Richard Wagner?
   - d. Giacomo Puccini?

9. **What instrument does Daniel Barenboim play?**
   Is it:
   - a. The cello?
   - b. The guitar?
   - c. The piano?
   - d. The flute?

10. **What does the title of Mozart's opera *Così Fan Tutte* mean?**
    Is it:
    - a. 'It's the same for everyone'?
    - b. 'So do all women'?
    - c. 'A comfortable living-room'?
    - d. 'We all fan ourselves'?

# A MIXED BAG

1. **What is a female badger called?**
   Is it:
   - a. A vixen?
   - b. A sow?
   - c. A bitch?
   - d. A queen?

2. **How far is Easter Island from other land?**
   Is it:
   - a. 2400 km?
   - b. 3000 km?
   - c. 20 km?
   - d. 1550 km?

3. **What is myrrh?**
   Is it:
   - a. A root?
   - b. A resin?
   - c. A leaf?
   - d. A flower?

4. **How many so-called 'Aubrey' stones are there at Stonehenge?**
   Are there:
   - a. Thirty-two?
   - b. Fifty-six?
   - c. Eighty?
   - d. Sixteen?

5. **What is a mutchkin?**
   Is it:
   - a. An Irish elf?
   - b. A Scottish liquid measurement?
   - c. A small Welsh mountain hut used by hikers?
   - d. A linen cap?

6. **What is the political status of Tunisia?**
   **Is it:**
      a. A kingdom?
      b. A French protectorate?
      c. A republic?
      d. A protected territory?
7. **Where is the Minack Theatre?**
   **Is it:**
      a. In London?
      b. In Edinburgh?
      c. In King's Lynn?
      d. In Porthcurno?
8. **Who invented the miners' safety lamp?**
   **Was it:**
      a. Sir Humphry Davy?
      b. Elias Ashmole?
      c. Sir Peter Lely?
      d. Robert Hooke?
9. **What is the county town of Essex?**
   **Is it:**
      a. Shoeburyness?
      b. Brentwood?
      c. Chelmsford?
      d. Leigh-on-Sea?
10. **Where is the former home of sculptor Dame Barbara Hepworth, now a museum and art gallery?**
    **Is it in:**
      a. St Ives?
      b. Herstmonceux?
      c. Shanklin?
      d. Chertsey?

# FUNNY PECULIAR

1. **What bizarre occurrence marked the first balloon crossing of the English Channel?**
   Was it:
       a. The balloon sank, and its passengers had to swim ashore?
       b. The balloon almost landed on the head of a French dignitary?
       c. The passengers had to jettison their clothes and so arrived naked?
       d. The balloon was impounded by the passengers' creditors?

2. **Mary, Queen of Scots, had the same bust measurement as a Hollywood sex symbol. Which one?**
   Was it:
       a. Jean Harlow?
       b. Mae West?
       c. Marilyn Monroe?
       d. Jayne Mansfield?

3. **Forbidden to keep a dog at his Cambridge college, Lord Byron kept another animal instead. What was it?**
   Was it:
       a. A pig?
       b. A horse?
       c. A bear?
       d. A monkey?

4. **A female mosquito can produce an enormous number of offspring in a year. How many?**
   Is it:
       a. 1,000,000?
       b. 5,000,000?
       c. 50,000,000?
       d. 150,000,000?

5. **Which planet is the only one to rotate clockwise?**
   Is it:
   - a. Venus?
   - b. Mars?
   - c. Mercury?
   - d. Jupiter?

6. **How many countries have no coastline?**
   Is it:
   - a. Twelve?
   - b. Seventeen?
   - c. Twenty-six?
   - d. Thirty-nine?

7. **What was named after Theodore Roosevelt?**
   Was it:
   - a. A rose?
   - b. A toy?
   - c. A dessert?
   - d. A hat?

8. **How fast can an ostrich run?**
   Is it:
   - a. 28 mph/45 kph?
   - b. 35 mph/56 kph?
   - c. 40 mph/64 kph?
   - d. 45 mph/72 kph?

9. **A famous film star caused a dramatic fall in the sale of vests in the USA when he revealed that he didn't wear one. Who was he?**
   Was he:
   - a. Rudolf Valentino?
   - b. Kirk Douglas?
   - c. Clark Gable?
   - d. Marlon Brando?

10. **Who wrote: 'Smoking is a custom loathsome to the eye, hateful to the nose, harmful to the brain, dangerous to the lungs.'?**
   - a. Edwina Currie?
   - b. Queen Victoria?
   - c. King James I?
   - d. Dr Edith Summerskill?

# A MIXED BAG

1. **Which football team's home ground is Goodison Park? Is it:**
   - a. Wolverhampton Wanderers?
   - b. Chelsea?
   - c. Leeds United?
   - d. Everton?

2. **What does 'inver' mean in Scottish place-names? Is it:**
   - a. A loch?
   - b. A mountain?
   - c. A village?
   - d. A river mouth?

3. **Who is Bryony Brind? Is she:**
   - a. A ballet dancer?
   - b. A sculptor?
   - c. An actress?
   - d. A pop singer?

4. **Where in the human body is the fibula? Is it part of:**
   - a. The arm?
   - b. The leg?
   - c. The chest?
   - d. The back?

5. **How old was Donald Duck in 1988? Was he:**
   - a. 40?
   - b. 48?
   - c. 54?
   - d. 62?

6. **When is St Nicholas's Day?**
   Is it:
       a. 6 December?
       b. 13 December?
       c. 20 December?
       d. 6 January?

7. **When was the Challenger space shuttle disaster?**
   Was it in:
       a. December 1985?
       b. January 1986?
       c. February 1986?
       d. March 1986?

8. **Which union was expelled from the TUC in September 1988?**
   Was it:
       a. The TGWU?
       b. The NUPE?
       c. The NUM?
       d. The EEPTU?

9. **In which country is the *krona* the unit of currency?**
   Is it in:
       a. Norway?
       b. Sweden?
       c. Denmark?
       d. Finland?

10. **What was the first name of Agatha Christie's elderly lady detective, Miss Marple?**
       a. Alice?
       b. Patience?
       c. Jane?
       d. Doris?

# CREEPY CRAWLIES

1. **What kind of creature is a devil's coach-horse?**
   Is it:
   - a. A spider?
   - b. A fly?
   - c. An earwig?
   - d. A beetle?

2. **How long does a queen honey bee live?**
   Is it:
   - a. One year?
   - b. Two to three years?
   - c. Four to five years?
   - d. Six to eight years?

3. **What do ladybirds feed on?**
   Is it:
   - a. Aphids?
   - b. Cabbage leaves?
   - c. Rose petals?
   - d. Frog hoppers?

4. **Comma, meadow brown and heath fritillaries are all kinds of what?**
   Are they:
   - a. Beetles?
   - b. Grasshoppers?
   - c. Moths?
   - d. Butterflies?

5. **How big is the biggest spider in the British Isles?**
   Is its leg span approximately:
   - a. 3.5 ins (89 millimetres)?
   - b. 4.5 ins (114 millimetres)?
   - c. 5.5 ins (140 millimetres)?
   - d. 6.5 ins (165 millimetres)?

6. **From what do bees make honey?**
   Is it:
   - a. Pollen?
   - b. Nectar?
   - c. Sap?
   - d. Bee eggs?

7. **Which of the insects below is the fastest flying?**
   Is it:
   - a. The dragonfly?
   - b. The housefly?
   - c. The wasp?
   - d. The bee?

8. **What is the commonest insect in the world?**
   Is it:
   - a. The housefly?
   - b. The woodlouse?
   - c. The flea?
   - d. The springtail?

9. **How many times its own height can a flea jump?**
   Is it approximately:
   - a. 50 times?
   - b. 80 times?
   - c. 100 times?
   - d. 130 times?

10. **What is the largest insect in the British Isles?**
    Is it:
    - a. The stag beetle?
    - b. The great diving beetle?
    - c. The death's head hawkmoth?
    - d. The swallowtail butterfly?

# A MIXED BAG

1. **How deep can a sea lion dive?**
   Is it:
   - a. 500 metres?
   - b. 50 metres?
   - c. 10 metres?
   - d. 100 metres?

2. **What is Manhattan?**
   Is it:
   - a. A city?
   - b. A state?
   - c. An island?
   - d. A province?

3. **Which is the most common bird of prey in Britain?**
   Is it:
   - a. Eagle?
   - b. Hawk?
   - c. Falcon?
   - d. Kestrel?

4. **At the time of the US Confederation, how many states were there?**
   Were there:
   - a. Five?
   - b. Fifty-one?
   - c. Thirteen?
   - d. Thirty-two?

5. **Who was the last Holy Roman Emperor?**
   Was it:
   - a. Charles V?
   - b. Napoleon?
   - c. Francis II?
   - d. Francis IV?

6. **What is Isle Royale?**
   Is it:
   - a. A USA island in Lake Superior?
   - b. An island in the Seine, near Paris?
   - c. An island that is a wildlife sanctuary in Upper Volta?
   - d. A Canadian island in the St Lawrence River?

7. **When did Al Jolson star in *The Jazz Singer*?**
   Was it:
   - a. 1927?
   - b. 1934?
   - c. 1924?
   - d. 1940?

8. **What does *ipso facto* mean?**
   Is it:
   - a. So be it?
   - b. By that very fact?
   - c. The same as?
   - d. Not factually proven?

9. **What percentage of weddings in Britain were recorded on video in 1987?**
   Was it:
   - a. 5%?
   - b. 53%?
   - c. 15%?
   - d. 42%?

10. **Who won the 100th men's finals at Wimbledon in 1986?**
    Was it:
    - a. Ivan Lendl?
    - b. Pat Cash?
    - c. Boris Becker?
    - d. Jimmy Connors?

# POETRY CORNER

1. **Who wrote:**
   **'My name is Ozymandias, king of kings:**
   **Look on my works, ye Mighty, and despair!'?**
   **Was it:**
   - a. William Shakespeare?
   - b. Lord Byron?
   - c. Percy Bysshe Shelley?
   - d. Robert Browning?

2. **What, in John Betjeman's poem, was Miss Joan Hunter Dunn doing when she was 'Furnish'd and burnish'd by Aldershot sun'?**
   **Was it:**
   - a. Playing golf?
   - b. Playing tennis?
   - c. Playing croquet?
   - d. Laying the tea table on the lawn?

3. **To whom did the Ancient Mariner tell his Rime?**
   **Was it:**
   - a. A sea captain?
   - b. A young sailor?
   - c. A priest?
   - d. A wedding guest?

4. **Who wrote: 'If I should die, think only this of me:**
   **That there's some corner of a foreign field**
   **That is forever England.'?**
   **Was it:**
   - a. Rupert Brooke?
   - b. Wilfred Owen?
   - c. Siegfried Sassoon?
   - d. Edward Thomas?

5. **What is the name of the W.B. Yeats poem that ends:
'Tread softly because you tread on my dreams.'?**
Was it:
   a. 'The Rose of the World'?
   b. 'When You Are Old'?
   c. 'The Lake Isle of Innisfree'?
   d. 'He Wishes for the Cloths of Heaven'?

6. **Who wrote the poem that begins: 'Season of mists and mellow fruitfulness . . .'?**
Was it:
   a. John Keats?
   b. Percy Bysshe Shelley?
   c. William Wordsworth?
   d. Lord Byron?

7. **Where did the snake which came to D.H. Lawrence's water trough live?**
Was it:
   a. Spain?
   b. Sicily?
   c. Greece?
   d. Australia?

8. **In which Shakespeare play are the lines:
'I know a bank whereon the wild thyme blows
Where oxlips and the nodding violet grows . . .'?**
Was it:
   a. *A Midsummer Night's Dream*?
   b. *Romeo and Juliet*?
   c. *As You Like It*?
   d. *Twelfth Night*?

9. **Who wrote the words of the song: 'So We'll Go No More A Roving'?**
Was it:
   a. William Shakespeare?
   b. Thomas Hardy?
   c. Lord Byron?
   d. W.H. Davies?

**10. How did the Lady of Shalott enter Camelot in Tennyson's poem?**
Was it:

        a. Riding in a golden carriage?
        b. Riding on Sir Lancelot's horse?
        c. Sailing in a shallop?
        d. Floating, dead, in a boat down the river?

# A MIXED BAG

1. **What colours are the Swedish flag?**
   **Are they:**
   - a. Bright blue and white?
   - b. Red, white and blue?
   - c. Red and white?
   - d. Light blue and yellow?

2. **Who lives in Thatched House Lodge, Richmond Park?**
   **Is it:**
   - a. Prince and Princess Michael of Kent?
   - b. The Duke and Duchess of Kent?
   - c. The Duke and Duchess of York?
   - d. Princess Alexandra and the Hon. Angus Ogilvy?

3. **What does the company Charbonnel et Walker specialise in?**
   **Is it:**
   - a. Wines?
   - b. Cheeses?
   - c. Chocolates?
   - d. Men's clothing?

4. **In which sport is the Londonderry Cup awarded?**
   **Is it in:**
   - a. Tennis?
   - b. Table tennis?
   - c. Badminton?
   - d. Squash?

5. **What is the capital of the Federal Republic of Germany?**
   **Is it:**
   - a. Bonn?
   - b. West Berlin?
   - c. East Berlin?
   - d. Leipzig?

6. **What is *kvass*?**
   Is it:
   - a. A drink made from mares' milk?
   - b. A South African stockade?
   - c. A fissure in the ice of a glacier?
   - d. A Russian alcoholic drink?

7. **La Scala in Milan is a famous opera house. What does its name mean?**
   Is it:
   - a. The scales?
   - b. The octave?
   - c. The stalls?
   - d. The staircase?

8. **What game do the New York Yankees play?**
   Is it:
   - a. American football?
   - b. Baseball?
   - c. Basketball?
   - d. Ice hockey?

9. **Where did Nelson sail from in the *Victory*?**
   Was it:
   - a. Portsmouth?
   - b. Southampton?
   - c. Plymouth?
   - d. London?

10. **In which language does *stisibo* mean thank you?**
   - a. Finnish?
   - b. Norwegian?
   - c. Russian?
   - d. Swahili?

# THE BODY BEAUTIFUL

1. **In which part of the body are the atlas and axis bones?**
   Are they in:
   - a. The neck?
   - b. The foot?
   - c. The hip girdle?
   - d. The wrist?

2. **How many chambers are there in the heart?**
   Are there:
   - a. One?
   - b. Two?
   - c. Three?
   - d. Four?

3. **What is the talus?**
   Is it:
   - a. A small bone in the ear?
   - b. A small bone in the ankle
   - c. A muscle in the arm?
   - d. A gland in the stomach?

4. **What is the weight of an adult human liver?**
   Is it approximately:
   - a. 1.5 pounds/680 grams?
   - b. 3 pounds/1530 grams?
   - c. 4.5 pounds/2211 grams?
   - d. 6 pounds/2721 grams?

5. **What is the aorta?**
   Is it:
   - a. A nerve in the leg?
   - b. The tube through which air passes from the nose to the lungs?
   - c. A tube from a kidney to the bladder?
   - d. The chief artery of the body?

6. **Which one of the following is not a muscle in the leg?**
   Is it:

       a. Soleus?
       b. Triceps?
       c. Gracilis?
       d. Gastrocnemius?

7. **Where is the sacro-iliac joint?**
   Is it:

       a. In the shoulder?
       b. In the skull?
       c. In the ankle?
       d. In the hip?

8. **What does the adjective 'renal' mean?**
   Is it:

       a. Concerned with the kidneys?
       b. Concerned with the liver?
       c. Concerned with the stomach?
       d. Concerned with the lungs?

9. **What is the peritoneum?**
   Is it:

       a. A membrane lining the abdominal cavity?
       b. A membrane surrounding the lungs?
       c. The muscular wall between the stomach and lungs?
       d. A tube between the stomach and intestines?

10. **Which gland in the body controls the function of most of the others?**
    Is it:

        a. The thyroid?
        b. The thymus?
        c. The pituitary?
        d. The parotid?

# A MIXED BAG

1. **Which was the first house in Britain to be run by hydro-electricity?**
   Was it:
   - a. Torosay Castle, Isle of Mull?
   - b. Cragside House, Rothbury, Morpeth?
   - c. Linley Sambourne House, 18 Stafford Terrace, London?
   - d. Penrhyn Castle, Bangor, Gwynedd?

2. **What is a tapster?**
   Is it:
   - a. A tap dancer?
   - b. A person who pulls ale?
   - c. A hamster?
   - d. A plumber with advanced training?

3. **When was Charlie Chaplin born?**
   Was it:
   - a. 1900?
   - b. 1910?
   - c. 1889?
   - d. 1920?

4. **Cruse is an organisation formed to help which group of people?**
   Is it:
   - a. People suffering from multiple sclerosis?
   - b. People in difficulty at sea?
   - c. People who have been unemployed for more than two years?
   - d. The widowed and their children?

5. **How many does 'myriad' mean?**
   Is it:
   - a. 1000 million?
   - b. 10 million?
   - c. Innumerable?
   - d. A million million?

6. **Who said 'There's a sucker born every minute.'?**
   Was it:
   - a. Lord Randolph Churchill?
   - b. Henry Ford?
   - c. Lee Iacocca?
   - d. P.T. Barnum?

7. **How many theatres are there in the National Theatre?**
   Are there:
   - a. One?
   - b. Four?
   - c. Three?
   - d. Two?

8. **Where was Isaac Newton born?**
   Was it:
   - a. Bunratty Castle, Co Clare?
   - b. Townend, Troutbeck, Cumbria?
   - c. Woolsthorpe Manor, Colsterworth?
   - d. The Old House, High Town, Hereford?

9. **What is muscat?**
   Is it:
   - a. A wild cat?
   - b. A mushroom?
   - c. A fur?
   - d. A grape?

10. **Where are the Catskill Mountains?**
    Are they in:
    - a. Canada?
    - b. New Zealand?
    - c. Bulgaria?
    - d. The USA?

# AS THEY SAY IN THE USA

1. **What is an eggplant?**
   **Is it:**
      a. A type of tomato?
      b. A kind of lettuce?
      c. A pepper?
      d. An aubergine?

2. **What does public school mean?**
   **Is it:**
      a. A private school?
      b. A municipal school?
      c. A school for the handicapped?
      d. A school that is part private, part municipal?

3. **What is smoked picnic shoulder?**
   **Is it:**
      a. Bacon fat?
      b. Slipper of bacon?
      c. Boned loin of pork?
      d. Belly of pork?

4. **Zucchini refers to what vegetable?**
   **Is it:**
      a. A courgette?
      b. A pumpkin?
      c. An olive?
      d. A pepper?

5. **In carpentry, what is a backsaw?**
   **Is it:**
      a. A bandsaw?
      b. A tenon saw?
      c. A hacksaw?
      d. A jigsaw?

6. **Duplex refers to what type of dwelling?**
   Is it:
   - a. A flat?
   - b. A small flat for first-time buyers?
   - c. A maisonette?
   - d. A shared flat?

7. **What is kerosene?**
   Is it:
   - a. Petrol?
   - b. Sealing wax?
   - c. Paraffin?
   - d. Diesel fuel?

8. **What does weather stripping mean?**
   Is it:
   - a. Removing old paint?
   - b. Sunbathing?
   - c. Turning off the central heating in summer?
   - d. A draught excluder?

9. **If someone refers to your John Hancock, what do they mean?**
   It is:
   - a. Your right hand?
   - b. Your mouth?
   - c. Your face?
   - d. Your signature?

10. **What is a subway?**
    Is it:
    - a. An underground walkway?
    - b. A subterranean sewer?
    - c. A road under a motorway?
    - d. A tube or underground railway?

# A MIXED BAG

1. **What is the Queen's second name?**
   Is it:
   - a. Mary?
   - b. Alexandra?
   - c. Victoria?
   - d. Anne?

2. **What is the chief colour of the MacLeod tartan?**
   Is it:
   - a. Red?
   - b. Green?
   - c. Blue?
   - d. Yellow?

3. **When does the Chelsea Flower Show take place?**
   Is it in:
   - a. April?
   - b. May?
   - c. June?
   - d. July?

4. **When did Winston Churchill die?**
   Was it:
   - a. 1975?
   - b. 1965?
   - c. 1963?
   - d. 1945?

5. **Who invented the thermometer?**
   Was it:
   - a. Charles Wheatstone?
   - b. Benjamin Franklin?
   - c. Alexander Graham Bell?
   - d. Galileo Galilei?

6. **In which US state is Tallahassee?**
   **Is it in:**
   - a. Florida?
   - b. Texas?
   - c. Mississippi?
   - d. Kentucky?

7. **Of what is Pb the chemical symbol?**
   **Is it:**
   - a. Plutonium?
   - b. Platinum?
   - c. Lead?
   - d. Iron?

8. **What colour is lapis lazuli?**
   **Is it:**
   - a. Green?
   - b Purple?
   - c. Turquoise?
   - d. Deep blue?

9. **What is the largest island in the world, excluding Australia?**
   **Is it:**
   - a. New Guinea?
   - b. Greenland?
   - c. Great Britain?
   - d. Borneo?

10. **What is the county town of Surrey?**
    **Is it:**
    - a. Guildford?
    - b. Kingston-upon-Thames?
    - c. Dorking?
    - d. Croydon?

# GETTING THERE

1. **If you were travelling by train from London to Wolverhampton, from which station would you travel? Would it be from?**
    a. St Pancras?
    b. King's Cross?
    c. Euston?
    d. Paddington?

2. **Which main road runs between Exeter and Plymouth? Is it:**
    a. The A30?
    b. The A38?
    c. The A39?
    d. The A390?

3. **What is the shortest sea crossing from Great Britain to Ireland? Is it:**
    a. Liverpool to Dublin?
    b. Holyhead to Dun Loghaire?
    c. Fishguard to Rosslare?
    d. Stranraer to Larne?

4. **If you were travelling on the London Underground from Harrow and Wealdstone to Oxford Circus, by which line would you travel? Would it be:**
    a. The Metropolitan Line?
    b. The Piccadilly Line?
    c. The Bakerloo Line?
    d. The Northern Line?

5. If you were travelling directly from Scarborough to Leeds, which of these towns or cities would you pass through?
Would you pass through:
- a. York?
- b. Harrogate?
- c. Great Driffield?
- d. Thirsk?

6. In which British city are Victoria and Piccadilly main line stations?
Are they in:
- a. London?
- b. Manchester?
- c. Liverpool?
- d. Glasgow?

7. From which port would you board a car ferry for Bergen?
Would it be:
- a. Aberdeen?
- b. Harwich?
- c. Hull?
- d. Newcastle?

8. If you were travelling from Oxford to Worcester by train, which of these towns would you pass through?
Would you pass through:
- a. Cheltenham?
- b. Chipping Norton?
- c. Evesham?
- d. Stratford-upon-Avon?

9. If you were travelling from Winchester to Salisbury, which river would you cross?
Would it be:
- a. The Test?
- b. The Kennet?
- c. The Thames?
- d. The Arun?

10. If you were sailing up the East Anglian coast from Southend to Great Yarmouth, in which order would you pass the following towns?
    a. Aldeburgh?
    b. Harwich?
    c. Clacton-on-Sea?
    d. Lowestoft?

# A MIXED BAG

1. **What is the barysphere?**
   **Is it:**
   a. A half of the terrestrial globe?
   b. The central portion of the Earth?
   c. The gaseous layer around the world?
   d. The atmosphere layer between the troposphere and the mesosphere?

2. **When was the portrait painter Thomas Gainsborough born?**
   **Was it:**
   a. 1727?
   b. 1803?
   c. 1920?
   d. 1809?

3. **What are Eurodollars?**
   **Are they:**
   a. Eurocheques?
   b. US dollars in a European holding for short-term finance?
   c. A loan to the EEC in Hong Kong dollars?
   d. Dollars which can be used only in EEC countries?

4. **Where is Gabon?**
   **Is it in:**
   a. Asia?
   b. Africa?
   c. Central America?
   d. The Philippines?

5. **Who purchased London's famous Old Vic theatre and renovated it?**
   Was it:
   - a. Prince Charles?
   - b. Ed Mirvish?
   - c. Sir Peter Hall?
   - d. Rupert Murdoch?

6. **Who invented the diesel engine?**
   Was it:
   - a. Rudolf Diesel?
   - b. Henry Ford?
   - c. Thomas Edison?
   - d. Alexander Graham Bell?

7. **What is dypsnoea?**
   Is it:
   - a. An affliction of the bowels?
   - b. Difficult or laboured breathing?
   - c. Relaxed breathing?
   - d. An artificial prose style?

8. **Who or what is/was Good King Henry?**
   Is/was it:
   - a. Henry I?
   - b. Henry VIII?
   - c. A plant?
   - d. A nickname for one of the first automobiles?

9. **What causes athlete's foot?**
   Is it:
   - a. A fungal infection?
   - b. A virus?
   - c. A chronic infection?
   - d. A bacterial infection?

10. **Where is the headquarters of the Automobile Association?**
    Is it in:
    - a. Basingstoke?
    - b. London?
    - c. Liverpool?
    - d. Norwich?

# ADJECTIVAL ANALYSIS

1. **What does quixotic mean?**
   Is it:
   - a. Fast-moving?
   - b. Idealistic?
   - c. Romantic?
   - d. Foreign?

2. **What does enervating mean?**
   Is it:
   - a. Providing sustenance?
   - b. Numbing?
   - c. Weakening?
   - d. Providing energy?

3. **What does disingenuous mean?**
   Is it:
   - a. Worldly?
   - b. Naive?
   - c. Truthful?
   - d. Insincere?

4. **What does sempiternal mean?**
   Is it:
   - a. Spring-like?
   - b. Everlasting?
   - c. Rural?
   - d. Cave-like?

5. **What does pixilated mean?**
   Is it:
   - a. Bewitched?
   - b. Bewildered?
   - c. Supernatural?
   - d. Pollinated?

6.  **What does vainglorious mean?**
    **Is it:**
    - a. Boastful?
    - b. Worthless?
    - c. Ignominious?
    - d. Successful?

7.  **What does exiguous mean?**
    **Is it:**
    - a. Scanty?
    - b. Necessary?
    - c. Relevant?
    - d. Out-going?

8.  **What does inchoate mean?**
    **Is it:**
    - a. Without means of communication?
    - b. Of a dark blue colour?
    - c. Cluttered?
    - d. Undeveloped?

9.  **What does bucolic mean?**
    **Is it:**
    - a. Drunk?
    - b. Pain-giving?
    - c. Pastoral?
    - d. Stubborn?

10. **What does jejune mean?**
    **Is it:**
    - a. Amusing?
    - b. Childish?
    - c. Of the consistency of jelly?
    - d. Concerned with the intestines?

# A MIXED BAG

1.  **Whom did Bessie Wallis Warfield Simpson marry? Was it:**
    a. President Roosevelt?
    b. Winston Churchill?
    c. King Edward VII?
    d. The Duke of Windsor?

2.  **What is the square root of 361? Is it:**
    a. 13?
    b. 17?
    c. 19?
    d. 23?

3.  **What is the common name of the antirrhinum? Is it:**
    a. A wallflower?
    b. An aster?
    c. A snapdragon?
    d. Love-in-a-mist?

4.  **What do the Swiss Guards do? Do they:**
    a. Form a guard of honour at the Vatican?
    b. Form a guard of honour for a visiting sovereign or head of state?
    c. Form a guard of honour at the Parliament in Berne?
    d. Form a guard of honour at the Royal Palace in Monaco?

5.  **What is the capital city of Syria? Is it:**
    a. Baghdad?
    b. Amman?
    c. Beirut?
    d. Damascus?

6. **What does DOC stand for?**
   Is it:
   - a. Distinguished Order of Chivalry?
   - b. Debt or credit?
   - c. Denominazione d'origine controllata?
   - d. Dame of Canada?
7. **What are Ayrshires, Dexters, Gloucesters and Galloways?**
   Are they:
   - a. Breeds of cattle?
   - b. Breeds of sheep?
   - c. Breeds of goat?
   - d. Types of sweaters?
8. **In which Christmas carol is the line, 'All meanly wrapp'd in swaddling bands'?**
   Is it in:
   - a. 'O Come, All Ye Faithful'?
   - b. 'Hark! The Herald Angels Sing'?
   - c. 'Away in a Manger'?
   - d. 'While Shepherds Watched Their Flocks By Night'?
9. **Who starred with Gary Cooper in *High Noon*?**
   Was it:
   - a. Grace Kelly?
   - b. Eva Marie Saint?
   - c. Katharine Hepburn?
   - d. Jane Russell?
10. **In which county is Andover?**
    Is it in:
    - a. Sussex?
    - b. Surrey?
    - c. Hampshire?
    - d. Berkshire?

# FEATHERED FRIENDS

1. **Which one of the following birds does not migrate?**
   Is it:
   - a. The cuckoo?
   - b. The barn owl?
   - c. The swift?
   - d. The Manx shearwater?

2. **Which is Britain's smallest bird?**
   Is it:
   - a. The wren?
   - b. The siskin?
   - c. The coal tit?
   - d. The goldcrest?

3. **What is a raptor?**
   It is:
   - a. A bird of prey which eats birds and small mammals?
   - b. A fish-eating bird?
   - c. An insect-eating bird?
   - d. A perching bird?

4. **Which bird forms the logo of the Royal Society for the Protection of Birds?**
   - a. The osprey?
   - b. The oystercatcher?
   - c. The curlew?
   - d. The avocet?

5. **Which one of the following birds is not a member of the crow family?**
   Is it:
   - a. The woodpecker?
   - b. The magpie?
   - c. The jackdaw?
   - d. The jay?

6. **The male of which species of garden bird is distinguished by its black 'bib'?**
   Is it:

   a. The blue tit?
   b. The sparrow?
   c. The robin?
   d. The wren?

7. **Which is the largest bird in the world?**
   Is it:

   a. The albatross?
   b. The condor?
   c. The marabou stork?
   d. The ostrich?

8. **The spine-tailed swift is, in level flight, the fastest bird in the world. Approximately how fast can it fly?**
   Is it:

   a. 86 mph/138 kph?
   b. 96 mph/154 kph?
   c. 106 mph/170 kph?
   d. 126 mph/203 kph?

9. **Which species of bird might be Aylesbury, Muscovy, Pekin or Rouen?**
   Is it:

   a. Geese?
   b. Ducks?
   c. Bantams?
   d. Hens?

10. **In which species are the male and female called cob and pen?**
    Is it:

    a. Geese?
    b. Eagles?
    c. Pigeons?
    d. Swans?

# A MIXED BAG

1. **What was the title of the direct heir to the French throne?**
   **Was it:**
   - a. The Crown Prince?
   - b. The Dauphin?
   - c. The Prince of All the French?
   - d. The Prince of Paris?

2. **Why is a tarantula spider so named?**
   **Is it named after:**
   - a. A town:
   - b. A banana?
   - c. A man?
   - d. A disease?

3. **Where is Aleppo?**
   **Is it in:**
   - a. Turkey?
   - b. Syria?
   - c. Iraq?
   - d. Iran?

4. **What is a cabal?**
   **Is it:**
   - a. A dried up river bed?
   - b. A small group of intriguers?
   - c. A witches' coven?
   - d. A gathering of wizards?

5. **When was Toulouse-Lautrec born?**
   **Was it:**
   - a. 1760?
   - b. 1864?
   - c. 1890?
   - d. 1903?

6. **What is a cuspidor?**
   - a. A spittoon?
   - b. The grinding surface of a tooth?
   - c. A flap on a heart valve?
   - d. Something shaped like a cusp?

7. **Where is the Great Dismal Swamp?**
   **Is it in:**
   - a. Ecuador?
   - b. Uganda?
   - c. Zambia?
   - d. The USA?

8. **When were The Rolling Stones formed as a rock group?**
   **Was it:**
   - a. 1962?
   - b. 1965?
   - c. 1959?
   - d. 1971?

9. **What weight of food does a killer whale eat every day?**
   **Is it:**
   - a. 10 kilos?
   - b. 7 kilos?
   - c. 130 kilos?
   - d. 68 kilos?

10. **Which city in North America has the largest Chinese population outside Hong Kong or China?**
    **Is it:**
    - a. Los Angeles?
    - b. Vancouver?
    - c. New York?
    - d. San Francisco?

# WHO SAID IT ?

1. Who wrote or said the following: 'Marriage has many pains, but celibacy has no pleasures.'?
   Was it:
   - a. Elizabeth I?
   - b. Samuel Pepys?
   - c. Dr Johnson?
   - d. Oliver Goldsmith?

2. Who wrote or said the following: 'Truth is rarely pure, and never simple.'?
   Was it:
   - a. Oscar Wilde?
   - b. Dorothy Parker?
   - c. Mrs Patrick Campbell?
   - d. George Bernard Shaw?

3. Who wrote or said the following: 'It is impossible to enjoy idling thoroughly unless one has plenty of work to do.'?
   Was it:
   - a. P.G. Wodehouse?
   - b. Jerome K. Jerome?
   - c. James Thurber?
   - d. Noël Coward?

4. Who wrote or said the following: 'History is bunk.'?
   Was it:
   - a. Henry Ford?
   - b. Charles de Gaulle?
   - c. Winston Churchill?
   - d. Arthur Scargill?

5. Who wrote or said the following: 'The two most beautiful words in the English language are "cheque enclosed".'?
Was it:

    a. W.C. Fields?
    b. Jack Benny?
    c. James Thurber?
    d. Dorothy Parker?

6. Who wrote or said the following: 'He who can, does. He who cannot, teaches.'?
Was it:

    a. G.K. Chesterton?
    b. George Bernard Shaw?
    c. Charles Dickens?
    d. Rudyard Kipling?

7. Who wrote or said the following: 'I used to be snow white . . . but I drifted.'?
Was it:

    a. Dorothy Parker?
    b. Mae West?
    c. Rita Hayworth?
    d. Doris Day?

8. Who wrote or said the following: 'I want there to be no peasant in my kingdom so poor that he cannot have a chicken in his pot every Sunday.'?
Was it:

    a. King Henri IV of France?
    b. Queen Elizabeth I?
    c. King Louis XIV of France?
    d. King Charles I?

9. Who wrote or said the following: 'London society is full of women of the very highest birth who have, of their own free choice, remained thirty-five for years.'?
Was it:

    a. Cecil Beaton?
    b. Noël Coward?
    c. Terence Rattigan?
    d. Oscar Wilde?

10. Who wrote or said the following: 'Public schools are the nurseries of all vice and immorality.'?
    Was it:
    - a. Tony Benn?
    - b. Henry Fielding?
    - c. John Wells?
    - d. Gyles Brandreth?

# A MIXED BAG

1.  **Which football team is known as the Spiders?**
    Is it:
    - a. Queen's Park Rangers?
    - b. Coventry City?
    - c. Sheffield United?
    - d. Leeds United?

2.  **Where are the Taunus Mountains?**
    Are they in:
    - a. Czechoslovakia?
    - b. Belgium?
    - c. East Germany?
    - d. West Germany?

3.  **Where are the Comoro Islands?**
    Are they in:
    - a. The Pacific Ocean?
    - b. The Indian Ocean?
    - c. The South Atlantic Ocean?
    - d. The South China Sea?

4.  **What was the name of Sir Francis Chichester's boat?**
    Was it called:
    - a. The *Mary Rose*?
    - b. The *Gipsy Moth*?
    - c. The *Bluebird*?
    - d. *Ocean Bound*?

5.  **In which Dickens novel does Uriah Heep appear?**
    Is it:
    - a. *Our Mutual Friend*?
    - b. *Nicholas Nickleby*?
    - c. *A Christmas Carol*?
    - d. *David Copperfield*?

**6. What is acetic acid better known as?**
Is it:

    a. Lemon juice?
    b. Vinegar?
    c. Aspirin?
    d. Tea?

**7. What is a Suffolk Punch?**
Is it:

    a. A type of boxing punch?
    b. A drink made from hot, spiced ale and apples?
    c. A heavy horse?
    d. A sideboard?

**8. Who was Henry VIII's third wife?**
Was she:

    a. Catherine of Aragon?
    b. Anne of Cleves?
    c. Anne Boleyn?
    d. Jane Seymour?

**9. In which city is the street called Unter den Linden?**
Is it in:

    a. Vienna?
    b. Berlin?
    c. Berne?
    d. Hamburg?

**10. What do young girls in Sweden do on St Lucia's Day?**
Do they:

    a. Put a sprig of rosemary under their pillows?
    b. Bake a special cake?
    c. Wear crowns of lighted candles?
    d. Go to bed without any supper?

# FEARSOME PHOBIAS

1. **What is ailurophobia?**
   **Is it fear of:**
   - a. Flying?
   - b. Illness?
   - c. Cats?
   - d. Insects?
2. **What is eremitophobia?**
   **Is it fear of:**
   - a. Singing?
   - b. Blushing?
   - c. Paying bills?
   - d. Solitude?
3. **What is brontophobia?**
   **Is it fear of?**
   - a. Dinosaurs?
   - b. Thunder?
   - c. Lung disease?
   - d. Nineteenth-century novels?
4. **What is phonophobia?**
   **Is it fear of:**
   - a. Speaking aloud?
   - b. Telephones?
   - c. Confined spaces?
   - d. Crowds?
5. **What is ophiophobia?**
   **Is it fear of:**
   - a. Music?
   - b. Madness?
   - c. Wearing rings?
   - d. Snakes?

6. **What is agoraphobia?**
   **Is it fear of:**
   - a. Open spaces?
   - b. Monkeys?
   - c. Rabbits?
   - d. Travel?

7. **What is theophobia?**
   **Is it fear of:**
   - a. The Bible?
   - b. God?
   - c. Dictionaries?
   - d. Philosophy?

8. **What is hygrophobia?**
   **Is it fear of:**
   - a. Horses?
   - b. Water?
   - c. Dampness?
   - d. Ponds?

9. **What is xenophobia?**
   **Is it fear of:**
   - a. Greeks?
   - b. Buddhism?
   - c. Foreigners?
   - d. X-rays?

10. **What is zoophobia?**
    **Is it fear of:**
    - a. Animals?
    - b. Fermentation?
    - c. Swallowing?
    - d. Zombies?

# A MIXED BAG

1. **Where are the Medway towns?**
   **Are they in:**
   - a. Suffolk?
   - b. Cumbria?
   - c. Kent?
   - d. Sussex?

2. **In which year did Barbra Streisand make *Funny Girl*?**
   **Was it:**
   - a. 1971?
   - b. 1972?
   - c. 1965?
   - d. 1968?

3. **What did the ancient Greeks and Romans use a strigil for?**
   **Was it:**
   - a. To eat snails?
   - b. To scrape the body after bathing?
   - c. To prepare the body for burial?
   - d. To write?

4. **Which one of the following was *not* a spa town?**
   **Was it:**
   - a. Bath?
   - b. Buxton?
   - c. Tunbridge Wells?
   - d. Reading?

5. **How many hills surround Rome?**
   **Is it:**
   - a. Ten?
   - b. Seven?
   - c. Three?
   - d. Two?

6.  **What title is the third son of the Sovereign traditionally given on his marriage?**
    Is it:

    a. Duke of Beaufort?
    b. Earl of Ulster?
    c. Prince Consort?
    d. Duke of Cambridge?

7.  **Which city has the second largest port in the UK?**
    Is it:

    a. Cardiff?
    b. Belfast?
    c. Manchester?
    d. Liverpool?

8.  **What is a *tableau vivant*?**
    Is it:

    a. A realistic movie?
    b. A picture posed by people?
    c. A colourfully laid out table?
    d. An exciting story?

9.  **What is meerschaum, the material used for making carved tobacco pipes?**
    Is it:

    a. Horn?
    b. Ivory?
    c. Mineral?
    d. Amber?

10. **Where is the British J.F. Kennedy memorial?**
    Is it:

    a. At Windsor Castle?
    b. In the foyer of the House of Commons?
    c. At Runnymede?
    d. In Grosvenor Square?

# OCEAN WAVES

1. **What is the largest sea in the world?**
   **Is it:**
   - a. The Mediterranean Sea?
   - b. The Bering Sea?
   - c. The Barents Sea?
   - d. The South China Sea?

2. **In which ocean is the island of St Helena?**
   **Is it:**
   - a. The South Pacific?
   - b. The South Atlantic?
   - c. The North Atlantic?
   - d. The Indian Ocean?

3. **What sea lies between Australia and New Zealand?**
   **Is it:**
   - a. The Indian Ocean?
   - b. The Coral Sea?
   - c. The Timor Sea?
   - d. The Tasman Sea?

4. **What area of the Earth's surface is covered by sea?**
   **Is it:**
   - a. 125,236,000 square miles/324,361,240 square kilometres?
   - b. 139,670,000 square miles/361,740,000 square kilometres?
   - c. 151,325,000 square miles/391,931,750 square kilometres?
   - d. 163,429,000 square miles/423,281,110 square kilometres?

5. **Which sea or ocean is bordered on the north by Pakistan, the west by Oman and the east by India?**
   Is it:
   - a. The Indian Ocean?
   - b. The Arabian Sea?
   - c. The Persian Gulf?
   - d. The Red Sea?

6. **What is the largest inland sea in the world?**
   Is it:
   - a. The Caspian Sea?
   - b. The Black Sea?
   - c. The Dead Sea?
   - d. The Aral Sea?

7. **Where is the Weddell Sea?**
   Is it:
   - a. East of Newfoundland?
   - b. Between Alaska and the USSR?
   - c. In the Arctic?
   - d. In the Antarctic?

8. **Which island(s) lie to the west of the Tyrrhenian Sea?**
   Is it/are they:
   - a. Corsica and Sardinia?
   - b. Sicily?
   - c. The Dodecanese?
   - d. The Balearic Islands?

9. **Where is the Denmark Strait?**
   Is it:
   - a. Between Denmark and Sweden?
   - b. Between Denmark and Norway?
   - c. Between Shetland and Norway?
   - d. Between Iceland and Greenland?

10. **Which is our largest ocean?**
    Is it:
    - a. The Pacific?
    - b. The Atlantic?
    - c. The Southern?
    - d. The Arctic?

# A MIXED BAG

1. **What percentage of British homes owns a television set?**
   Is it:
   - a. 75%?
   - b. 82%?
   - c. 92%?
   - d. 98%?

2. **When were the Red Arrows, the aerobatic display team, officially formed?**
   Was it:
   - a. 1952?
   - b. 1959?
   - c. 1965?
   - d. 1973?

3. **What is Blue John?**
   Is it:
   - a. A mountain in Wyoming?
   - b. A wild flower?
   - c. A flag?
   - d. A semi-precious stone?

4. **What kind of tree is a linden tree?**
   Is it:
   - a. A lime tree?
   - b. A poplar tree?
   - c. A birch tree?
   - d. An ash tree?

5. **When was Theodore Roosevelt president of the USA?**
   Was it:
   - a. 1898–1902?
   - b. 1901–9?
   - c. 1905–14?
   - d. 1910–17?

6. **Where might you spend a *zloty*?**
   **Might it be:**
   - a. In Czechoslovakia?
   - b. In Hungary?
   - c. In Poland?
   - d. In Romania?

7. **When did the Hundred Years' War start?**
   **Was it:**
   - a. In 1302?
   - b. In 1337?
   - c. In 1358?
   - d. In 1389?

8. **What colour are copper sulphate crystals?**
   **Are they:**
   - a. Blue?
   - b. Green?
   - c. White?
   - d. Reddish-brown?

9. **What day is Michaelmas?**
   **Is it:**
   - a. 30 August?
   - b. 1 September?
   - c. 29 September?
   - d. 1 October?

10. **In which London postal district is Piccadilly?**
    **Is it in:**
    - a. SW1?
    - b. W1?
    - c. EC1?
    - d. WC1?

# CEREMONIES AND CUSTOMS

1. **How old was 'the Ripon Hornblower' in 1986?**
   **Was he:**
   - a. An unknown age?
   - b. 500 years old?
   - c. 800 years old?
   - d. 1000 years old?

2. **Which event closes the Egremont Crab Fair?**
   **Is it:**
   - a. Climbing the greasy pole?
   - b. The Maypole Dance?
   - c. The Applecart Parade?
   - d. The Gurning Contest?

3. **What do the Grenoside Sword Dancers of Yorkshire do to their captain near the beginning of the dance?**
   **Do they:**
   - a. 'Decapitate' him?
   - b. Knock him down?
   - c. Carry him on their shoulders?
   - d. Throw him in the river?

4. **Which people originated the unique Abbots Bromley Horn Dancers?**
   - a. The Romans?
   - b. The Saxons?
   - c. Unknown?
   - d. The Vikings?

5. **Ancient wells were often worshipped. What offerings were made to the Scottish 'clootie' wells?**
   **Was it:**
   - a. Coins?
   - b. Flowers?
   - c. Pieces of cloth?
   - d. Herbs?

6. **How often does 'Riding the Bounds' at Richmond in Yorkshire occur?**
   Is it:
   - a. Every year?
   - b. Every seven years?
   - c. Every ten years?
   - d. Every twenty-five years?

7. **According to legend, in which years may the Whitby Penny Hedge *not* be built?**
   Is it:
   - a. When the tides are too high?
   - b. In uneven numbered years?
   - c. If there is a death in the family?
   - d. If the soil is too hard?

8. **What happens if someone in a mummers play is recognised?**
   Does it mean:
   - a. He is thrown out?
   - b. The 'luck' is broken?
   - c. The play ends?
   - d. He can never be in the play again?

9. **What event does the Lewes Bonfire Night commemorate?**
   Is it:
   - a. Hallowe'en?
   - b. The death of protestant martyrs?
   - c. Guy Fawkes?
   - d. A great fire which burned down most of the town?

10. **The Bury Man of Queensferry is covered all over in what material?**
    Is it:
    - a. Flowers?
    - b. Flags?
    - c. Burrs?
    - d. Scottish thistles?

# A MIXED BAG

1. **Which president died in an air crash in August 1988?**
   **Was it:**
   - a. President Marcos?
   - b. President Bhutto?
   - c. President Botha?
   - d. President Zia?

2. **Who wrote *The Secret Diary of Adrian Mole*?**
   **Was it:**
   - a. Roald Dahl?
   - b. Enid Blyton?
   - c. Sue Townsend?
   - d. Beverly Cleary?

3. **What is/was the *Karin B*?**
   **Is/was it:**
   - a. A ferry which sank in the Middle East?
   - b. An aircraft which crashed into a crowd of spectators?
   - c. A ship loaded with toxic waste?
   - d. The codename of an IRA plot?

4. **How many letters a day does the Post Office handle?**
   **Is it:**
   - a. 21,000,000?
   - b. 31,000,000?
   - c. 41,000,000?
   - d. 51,000,000?

5. **When was the Chernobyl disaster?**
   **Was it in:**
   - a. April 1985?
   - b. April 1986?
   - c. October 1986?
   - d. May 1987?

6. **What distinction did a dog called Ted have?**
   **Was it that he was:**
   - a. The first dog Mrs Thatcher owned?
   - b. The dog who saved Prince Harry from drowning?
   - c. The first dog Britain sent into space?
   - d. The first dog allowed into the House of Commons?

7. **When was the Great Fire of London?**
   **Was it in:**
   - a. 1536?
   - b. 1665?
   - c. 1666?
   - d. 1786?

8. **What is a cabbage white?**
   **Is it:**
   - a. A vegetable?
   - b. A butterfly?
   - c. A hat?
   - d. A disease of cabbages?

9. **Approximately how many acres has Hyde Park?**
   **Is it:**
   - a. 200?
   - b. 280?
   - c. 340?
   - d. 450?

10. **Which one of the following plants is not poisonous?**
    **Is it:**
    - a. The foxglove?
    - b. The laburnum?
    - c. The nasturtium?
    - d. The lily of the valley?

# AROUND BRITAIN

1.  **Between which cities does the M1 run?**
    **Is it between:**
    - a. London and Sheffield?
    - b. London and Leeds?
    - c. London and Newcastle?
    - d. London and Edinburgh?
2.  **Where is Mablethorpe?**
    **Is it:**
    - a. On the Lincolnshire coast?
    - b. On the Lancashire coast?
    - c. On the Norfolk coast?
    - d. On the Northumberland coast?
3.  **In which direction does Penzance face the sea?**
    **Is it:**
    - a. North?
    - b. South?
    - c. East?
    - d. West?
4.  **From where would you sail to Stornoway?**
    **Would you sail from:**
    - a. Kyle of Lochalsh?
    - b. Portree?
    - c. Oban?
    - d. Ullapool?
5.  **Which town is on the opposite side of the Tamar Bridge from Plymouth?**
    **Is it:**
    - a. Devonport?
    - b. Saltash?
    - c. Looe?
    - d. Salcombe?

6. **John O'Groats is the north-easterly point of Scotland. What is the north-westerly point called?**
   Is it:
   - a. Thurso?
   - b. Duncansby Head?
   - c. Sumburgh Head?
   - d. Cape Wrath?

7. **What is the name of the light railway that runs along the south coast of England?**
   Is it:
   - a. The Romney, Hythe and Dymchurch Railway?
   - b. The Hastings, Rye and Winchelsea Railway?
   - c. The Dover–Folkestone Railway?
   - d. The Bexhill, Pevensey, St Leonards Railway?

8. **Where is the Princess of Wales's ancestral home, Althorp House?**
   Is it:
   - a. Near Cheltenham?
   - b. Near Norwich?
   - c. Near Northampton?
   - d. Near Cambridge?

9. **Michael Parkinson's Barnsley is in South Yorkshire. Where in Britain is the other one?**
   Is it in:
   - a. North Yorkshire?
   - b. East Sussex?
   - c. Durham?
   - d. Gloucestershire?

10. **Where is the island of Bardsey?**
    Is it:
    - a. In the Outer Hebrides?
    - b. In the Orkneys?
    - c. Off the North Wales coast?
    - d. In the Scilly Isles?

# A MIXED BAG

1. **What is the maximum weight letter/package that can be posted first class for 19p (May 1989)?**
   Is it:
   - a. 50 grams?
   - b. 2 ounces?
   - c. 60 grams?
   - d. 100 grams?

2. **Who are Julian, Dick, Anne, George and Timmy?**
   Are they:
   - a. The first five satellites launched into space?
   - b. The Queen's corgis?
   - c. Jeffrey Archer's children?
   - d. The Famous Five characters created by Enid Blyton?

3. **Where is the Castle of Mey?**
   Is it:
   - a. Near John O'Groats?
   - b. In Northumberland?
   - c. On the north-west coast of Scotland?
   - d. On the Isle of Mull?

4. **Which great producer of racing cars died in August 1988?**
   Was it:
   - a. Colin Chapman?
   - b. Enzo Ferrari?
   - c. Ken Tyrrell?
   - d. Ettore Bugatti?

5. **What is Lucie Rie's profession?**
   Is she:
   - a. A painter?
   - b. A potter?
   - c. A writer?
   - d. A dancer?

6. **Against which country did England win a Test Match in the summer of 1988 after losing eighteen in a row?**
   Was it:
   - a. The West Indies?
   - b. India?
   - c. Australia?
   - d. Sri Lanka?

7. **Who lives at Gatcombe Park?**
   Is it:
   - a. The Princess Royal?
   - b. The Prince and Princess of Wales?
   - c. Prince and Princess Michael of Kent?
   - d. The Duke and Duchess of Gloucester?

8. **What are Lindsey, Kesteven and Holland?**
   Are they:
   - a. Types of cloth?
   - b. Types of brick?
   - c. Parts of Lincolnshire?
   - d. Rivers?

9. **Who owns Harrods?**
   Is it:
   - a. Grand Metropolitan Hotels?
   - b. The Al-Fayed brothers?
   - c. The House of Fraser?
   - d. HM The Queen?

10. **Where is the National Stud?**
    Is it in:
    - a. Lambourn?
    - b. Goodwood?
    - c. Epsom?
    - d. Newmarket?

# ABBREVIATIONS

What do these abbreviations stand for?

1. **ACAS?**
   Is it:
   a. Academy of Cheltenham and Stroud?
   b. Associate of the Clerical Administration Society?
   c. Advisory, Conciliation and Arbitration Service?
   d. Administrative Chartering of Admiralty Ships?

2. **RHS?**
   Is it:
   a. Royal Horticultural Society?
   b. Royal Horse Society?
   c. Regimental Honorary Sergeant?
   d. Railfreight Handling Service?

3. **Quango?**
   Is it:
   a. Qualified national government officers?
   b. Quasi-non-governmental organisation?
   c. Quantitive numerical galactic order?
   d. Quasi-nuclear generator observation?

4. **LRAM?**
   Is it:
   a. Licentiate of the Royal Academy of Music?
   b. London Regional Aircraft Museum?
   c. Lloyds Register of Ancient Mariners?
   d. Liverpool Royal Academy of Musicians?

5. **NASA?**
   Is it:
   a. National Administration of Space and Air?
   b. National Aeronautics and Space Administration?
   c. National Aviation and Space Academy?
   d. Naval Aircraft and Space Administration?

6. **ad. lib.?**
   Is it:

   - a. *ad liberatum* – at will?
   - b. *addendum libatio* – an extra offered free of charge?
   - c. *ad libra* – in the balance?
   - d. *ad libitum* – at pleasure?

7. **MI Mech E?**
   Is it?

   - a. Midlands Institute of Mechanical Engineers?
   - b. Manchester Inspectorate of Mechanics and Engineers?
   - c. Member of the Institute of Mechanical Engineers?
   - d. Metropolitan Institute of Mechanics and Engine-drivers?

8. **radar?**
   Is it:

   - a. Radio dispatches audio receiver?
   - b. Relay attention/detection arrangement?
   - c. Radio detection affirmation radius?
   - d. Radio detection and ranging?

9. **DNA?**
   Is it?

   - a. Deoxyribonucleic acid?
   - b. Died naturally on arrival?
   - c. Dover Navigation Association?
   - d. Dressmakers' and Needlewomen's Association?

10. **ARICS?**
    Is it:

    - a. Artists, Retouchers, Illustrators and Cartoonists Society?
    - b. Associate of the Royal Institute of Chartered Surveyors?
    - c. Association of Researchers, Investigators, Criminologists and Scrutineers?
    - d. Associate of the Royal Institute of Chartered Secretaries?

# A MIXED BAG

1.  **Who are Mel Smith and Griff Rhys Jones?**
    **Are they:**
    - a.  Television scriptwriters?
    - b.  Television comedians?
    - c.  Politicians?
    - d.  Radio personalities?

2.  **Malaria, whooping cough, measles, tetanus – what have these diseases in common?**
    **Is it that:**
    - a.  They all originated in Africa?
    - b.  They all must be notified to a medical officer for environmental health?
    - c.  They all affect the lungs?
    - d.  They are all diseases of childhood?

3.  **What is the normal human temperature in Centigrade?**
    **Is it:**
    - a.  34.8°C?
    - b.  35.8°C?
    - c.  36.8°C?
    - d.  37.8°C?

4.  **What colour period did Picasso move into after his Blue Period?**
    **Was it:**
    - a.  Red?
    - b.  Pink?
    - c.  Purple?
    - d.  Green?

5. Which 5 ft 4 in female tennis star said, 'If you're small, you'd better be a winner.'?
   Was it:
   - a. Maureen Connolly?
   - b. Evonne Goolagong?
   - c. Rosemary Casals?
   - d. Billie Jean King?

6. Which is the most widely spoken language in the world?
   Is it:
   - a. Hindustani?
   - b. English?
   - c. Standardised Northern Chinese?
   - d. Spanish?

7. Which British newspaper has the largest circulation?
   Is it:
   - a. *The Sun*?
   - b. The *Daily Mirror*?
   - c. The *Daily Express*?
   - c. The *News of the World*?

8. Who was Ernst Lubitsch?
   Was he:
   - a. A film director?
   - b. A politician?
   - c. A composer?
   - d. A sculptor?

9. Who wrote *The Brothers Karamazov*?
   Was it:
   - a. Tolstoy?
   - b. Dostoyevsky?
   - c. Turgenev?
   - d. Pasternak?

10. What did King George VI die of?
    Was it:
    - a. A heart attack?
    - b. Lung cancer?
    - c. Chronic bronchitis?
    - d. A cerebral thrombosis?

# RADIO TIME

1.  **Who presents *Woman's Hour* (1989)?**
    Is it:

    a. Sue MacGregor?
    b. Dilly Barlow?
    c. Jenni Murray?
    d. Margaret Howard?

2.  **At what time of the morning does Derek Jameson's Radio 2 show begin?**
    Is it:

    a. 6.30 am?
    b. 7.30 am?
    c. 8.30 am?
    d. 9.30 am?

3.  **With what is *Week Ending* concerned?**
    Is it about:

    a. The news?
    b. A review of the week's programmes?
    c. Comedy?
    d. Listeners' letters?

4.  **On which station is *Mainly for Pleasure*?**
    Is it on:

    a. Radio 1?
    b. Radio 2?
    c. Radio 3?
    d. Radio 4?

5.  **Who, in *The Archers*, lives at Home Farm?**
    Is it:

    a. Jill and Phil Archer?
    b. Pat and Tony Archer?
    c. Joe, Eddie and Clarrie Grundy?
    d. Brian and Jennifer Aldridge?

6. **Who presents *Bookshelf* (1989)?**
   Is it:
   - a. Nigel Forde?
   - b. George Macbeth?
   - c. Brian Gear?
   - d. John Humphrys?

7. **With what is *Kaleidoscope* concerned?**
   Is it:
   - a. The arts?
   - b. Science?
   - c. News?
   - d. Current affairs?

8. **Who presents *Desert Island Discs* (1989)?**
   Is it:
   - a. Gloria Hunniford?
   - b. Sue Lawley?
   - c. Michael Parkinson?
   - d. Libby Purves?

9. **During which hours does Radio 2 transmit?**
   Is it:
   - a. 5.30 am to midnight?
   - b. 5.30 am to 3 am?
   - c. 6.30 to 1 am?
   - d. Round the clock?

10. **Who Stops the Week on Saturday?**
    Is it:
    - a. Nigel Rees?
    - b. Robert Robinson?
    - c. Benny Green?
    - d. Jonathan Dimbleby?

# A MIXED BAG

1. **Where can the aurora borealis normally be seen?**
   Is it:
   - a. At the North Pole?
   - b. In the northern and southern hemispheres?
   - c. At the Equator?
   - d. At the South Pole?

2. **Which kind of pottery is fired to the highest temperature?**
   Is it:
   - a. Earthenware?
   - b. Stoneware?
   - c. Porcelain?
   - d. Table-to-oven ware?

3. **Which animal has the warmest fur known to man?**
   Is it:
   - a. Seal?
   - b. Fox?
   - c. Walrus?
   - d. Caribou?

4. **Who is the author of *The Cremation of Sam McGee*?**
   Is it:
   - a. Robert Louis Stevenson?
   - b. Robert Service?
   - c. Jeffrey Archer?
   - d. Pierre Burton?

5. **How many square kilometres of lakes are there in the province of Ontario, Canada?**
   Are there:
   - a. 3 sq km?
   - b. 30 sq km?
   - c. 70,000 sq km?
   - d. 177,000 sq km?

6. **What does stentorian mean?**
   Is it:
   - a. Standing still?
   - b. Like a stenographer?
   - c. Stern?
   - d. Loud?

7. **When was the Oxford and Cambridge Boat Race first held?**
   Was it:
   - a. 1829?
   - b. 1900?
   - c. 1964?
   - d. 1885?

8. **To whom do the swans between Sunbury and Pangbourne on the Thames belong?**
   Is it:
   - a. The Queen?
   - b. The Queen, the Dyers Company and the Vintners Company?
   - c. The Queen and the City of London?
   - d. No one?

9. **What does a philatelist collect?**
   Is it:
   - a. Coins?
   - b. Militaria?
   - c. Shells?
   - d. Stamps?

10. **What is Doggett's Coat and Badge?**
    Is it:
    - a. The Thames Boatmen's race?
    - b. A dog race held in Middlesbrough?
    - c. A style of fashion in the 1750s?
    - d. An award for the fastest boat crossing the Channel?

# THE PLAY'S THE THING

1. **On which play by George Bernard Shaw was the musical *My Fair Lady* based?**
   Was it:
   - a. *Arms and the Man*?
   - b. *Pygmalion*?
   - c. *Heartbreak House*?
   - d. *Major Barbara*?

2. **Who wrote *Uncle Vanya* and *The Three Sisters*?**
   Was it:
   - a. Harold Pinter?
   - b. Henrik Ibsen?
   - c. Alan Ayckbourn?
   - d. Anton Chekhov?

3. **In which play does Lady Bracknell appear?**
   Is it in:
   - a. *Lady Windermere's Fan*?
   - b. *Candida*?
   - c. *The Country Wife*?
   - d. *The Importance of Being Earnest*?

4. **Who wrote *The Beggar's Opera*?**
   Was it:
   - a. John Gay?
   - b. Bertolt Brecht?
   - c. John Vanbrugh?
   - d. Giuseppe Verdi?

5. **Which American playwright wrote *A Streetcar Named Desire* and *Cat on a Hot Tin Roof*?**
   Was it:
   - a. Tennessee Williams?
   - b. Arthur Miller?
   - c. Eugene O'Neill?
   - d. David Mamet?

6. Who wrote *Le Tartuffe*, *Le Misanthrope* and *Le Malade Imaginaire*?
   Was he:
   - a. Victor Hugo?
   - b. Racine?
   - c. Molière?
   - d. Jean Cocteau?

7. Who or what was the Admirable Crichton in the play of that name by J.M. Barrie?
   Was he, she or it:
   - a. A boat?
   - b. A butler?
   - c. A soldier?
   - d. A dog?

8. Who wrote *Volpone*, *Bartholomew Fair* and *The Alchemist*?
   Was it:
   - a. John Webster?
   - b. Beaumont and Fletcher?
   - c. Christopher Marlowe?
   - d. Ben Jonson?

9. Who wrote *The Way of the World*?
   Was it:
   - a. William Congreve?
   - b. Alexander Pope?
   - c. John Arbuthnot?
   - d. William Wycherley?

10. Which stage musical is based on Shakespeare's *The Taming of the Shrew*?
    Is it:
    - a. *Guys and Dolls*?
    - b. *Brigadoon*?
    - c. *The King and I*?
    - d. *Kiss Me, Kate*?

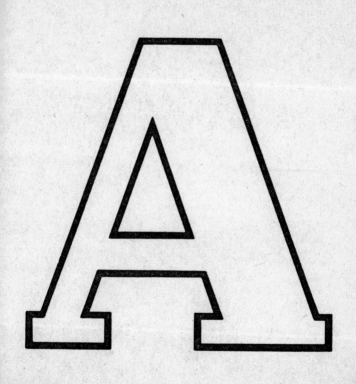

# 1000 ANSWERS

## A MIXED BAG page 13
1. The Queen Mother
2. 1 August
3. Gatwick
4. Dashiel Hammett
5. An architect
6. Windermere
7. Trees and forests
8. The UK's second highest mountain
9. New York
10. All have the suffix 'Regis'

## HOME, SWEET HOME page 15
1. Damp-proof course
2. A horizontal beam over a doorway or window frame
3. Outdoor plaster with an ornamental pattern
4. A course of brickwork which projects beyond the others
5. Square-cut stone
6. One of a row of short pillars
7. The horizontal bar of a window
8. The vertical bar between the panes of a window
9. Pointed at the top
10. A projection of timber or stone jutting out from a wall

## A MIXED BAG page 17
1. 6 feet
2. A guinea pig
3. Gnasher
4. An observatory in Cheshire
5. Sherlock Holmes
6. In London's Hyde Park
7. 212°F
8. Marmalade
9. All are sources of spring water
10. A sports commentator

## WINING AND DINING page 19
1. Sturgeon
2. Chateau d'Yquem
3. Cheeses
4. A wine waiter
5. Pancakes cooked with brandy and liqueur
6. A cocktail made from brandy and dry ginger, served with a piece of orange peel
7. A mixture of wine, oil, herbs and vegetables in which meat is soaked
8. Roquefort
9. A Provençal fish stew
10. Champagne

## A MIXED BAG page 21
1. A strangely shaped column of rock
2. An illustrator of children's books
3. Ireland
4. New York
5. A mathematical term
6. Bosham
7. A ship
8. The stigmas of crocus
9. A rod which shows the time
10. Henry VI

## THE SPORT OF KINGS page 23
1. The Jockey Club
2. Just over 4 miles (6 kilometres)
3. Four days
4. Doncaster
5. They are all races for fillies only
6. Kahyasi
7. The 2000 Guineas, the Derby and the St Leger
8. A trainer
9. He won the Grand National three times
10. Longchamp

## A MIXED BAG page 25
1. In the USSR
2. Sir Thomas Malory
3. The Thursday before Good Friday
4. Picasso
5. The writer Agatha Christie
6. Charon
7. Prince Charles
8. Sheffield
9. In the Kremlin
10. Their height

## ALL THE WORLD'S A STAGE page 27
1. The National Theatre
2. Henry Irving
3. *Chess*
4. The Whitehall
5. The Coliseum
6. Glasgow
7. Victor Hugo
8. *The Mousetrap*
9. Regent's Park
10. Her Majesty's Theatre

## A MIXED BAG page 29
1. A type of lace
2. 50
3. Sir Francis Drake
4. A North London newspaper
5. Superman
6. Tail
7. A castrated male sheep
8. St Christopher
9. Twelve
10. A carriage used in harness racing in the USA

## TOURISTS' EUROPE page 31
1. Amsterdam
2. Siena
3. Geneva
4. Rhodes
5. Vienna
6. The west
7. Venice
8. Granada
9. Simplon
10. Brussels

## A MIXED BAG page 33
1. Henry VIII
2. The International Monetary Fund
3. The Isles of Scilly
4. A fish
5. Title deeds
6. A horse or donkey
7. *The Woman in White*
8. A fabric
9. A lettuce
10. Brazil

## NUMBER, PLEASE page 35
1. Forty-five years
2. 94 miles (151 kilometres)
3. 50°F
4. £14,000,000
5. 63%
6. 457,500
7. Forty-six
8. The fifty-first
9. One car per two people
10. 38.5 million

## A MIXED BAG page 37
1. Hair dressing
2. Battle
3. A surveying instrument
4. Isaac Walton
5. Yellow
6. Inuit
7. Dublin
8. A contraption to slow down a vessel
9. A sleeping sickness
10. Salisbury

## THE HIGHWAY CODE page 39
1. 60 mph
2. Stop
3. Cycle route ahead
4. When someone is driving slowly on the right of the road looking for a turning
5. 60 mph
6. A warning to other road users of your presence
7. 315 feet (96 metres)
8. No motor vehicles except solo motorcycles, scooters or mopeds
9. Continue
10. 30 mph

## A MIXED BAG page 42
1. The Barbican
2. William Shakespeare's
3. Thirty
4. British
5. Fencing
6. Near the Bahamas
7. Devastated the Caribbean
8. Four sons and five daughters
9. Iceland
10. 58

## THE SILVER SCREEN page 44
1. *Nosferatu*
2. Greta Garbo
3. James Stewart
4. Bernardo Bertolucci
5. *Snow White and the Seven Dwarfs*
6. *On Her Majesty's Secret Service*
7. *The Misfits*
8. Bolivia
9. *South Pacific*
10. Diane Keaton

## A MIXED BAG page 46
1. 1883
2. Ely
3. A bird
4. Japan
5. Four sets per thousand births
6. Copper and tin
7. A cabbage
8. Fossilised resin
9. 1969
10. Matilda

## UNCLE SAM page 48
1. Fifty
2. Delaware
3. Kentucky
4. New Amsterdam
5. 1620
6. Third
7. Mount McKinley
8. Philadelphia
9. 1861–63
10. Jimmy Carter

## A MIXED BAG page 50
1. Kent
2. Travelling on foot
3. 1086
4. Dry scrubland, particularly in the south-eastern USA
5. West Ham United football team
6. A collar bone
7. An eighteenth-century Poet Laureate
8. India
9. An African antelope
10. The first man to make a powered flight across the English Channel

**SPELLING BEE** page 52
1. a. Incorrect: ambassador
   b. Correct
   c. Incorrect: carillon
   d. Incorrect: dalmatian
2. a. Correct
   b. Incorrect: fuchsia
   c. Incorrect: gynaecologist
   d. Incorrect: hypocrisy
3. a. Correct
   b. Incorrect: khaki
   c. Incorrect: impostor
   d. Correct
4. a. Correct
   b. Correct
   c. Incorrect: omission
   d. Correct
5. a. Incorrect: querulous
   b. Correct
   c. Correct
   d. Incorrect: toboggan
6. a. Correct
   b. Incorrect: vaccination
   c. Correct
   d. Correct
7. a. Incorrect: yodel
   b. Incorrect: zeppelin
   c. Correct
   d. Correct
8. a. Correct
   b. Incorrect: diarrhoea
   c. Incorrect: entrepreneur
   d. Correct
9. a. Incorrect: graffiti
   b. Incorrect: hieroglyphic
   c. Incorrect: idiosyncrasy
   d. Incorrect: jodhpurs
10. a. Incorrect: kapok
    b. Correct
    c. Correct
    d. Incorrect: nincompoop

**A MIXED BAG** page 54
1. The part of a cat's eye that apparently glows in the dark
2. Seven
3. Victorian
4. John Tenniel
5. Newfoundland
6. 1870
7. An optical navigational instrument
8. Rouen
9. A medieval instrument of torture
10. The head of a bull, body of a man

**WEAPONS OF WAR** page 56
1. A Japanese long sword
2. The inventor
3. At the end of the 14th century
4. Persia
5. 1915
6. The Colt-Browning of 1895
7. The Lee-Enfield No. 4
8. An early Scottish barrel gun
9. 1351–2
10. *Jambiya*

**A MIXED BAG** page 58
1. Kierkegaard
2. A variety of cabbage
3. The 800 metres, the 100 metres hurdles, the shot, the high hump and the long jump
4. Belgian
5. Somalia
6. An open-sided summer house
7. 8 December
8. Iron pyrites
9. Cycling
10. R.S. Surtees

## PRIME MINISTERS page 60

1. Five
2. 1830–34
3. The Earl of Rosebery
4. Bexley
5. Ramsay MacDonald
6. Bladon
7. Harold Wilson
8. Stanley Baldwin
9. Alec Douglas-Home
10. Winston Churchill

## A MIXED BAG page 62

1. A gas-operated clock
2. Tsar Alexander I
3. It was transported by sea
4. Japan
5. 10%
6. The Isle of Man
7. China
8. The Queen
9. 1964
10. A salamander

## GARDENERS' WORLD page 64

1. 7
2. Yellow, edged with pink
3. A runner bean
4. Love-in-a-mist
5. Early dessert apples
6. Hydrangea
7. Geranium
8. Blue
9. The larvae of crane flies
10. Clematis

## A MIXED BAG page 66

1. 4 ft 8½ in
2. The nearest group of stars to the Earth
3. Colorado beetle
4. A cook
5. 1903
6. Tennis
7. Orkney
8. Prince Charming's valet
9. A mountaineer
10. Goose

## PETS' CORNER page 68

1. 6 miles (9½ kilometres)
2. The cocker spaniel
3. A rabbit
4. The desert
5. The Canary Islands
6. Chestnut brown
7. Not more than three or four years, and often less
8. The young of a salamander
9. 6 miles d(9½ kilometres)
10. A cat

## A MIXED BAG page 70

1. The molten fluid within the Earth's crust
2. Fourteen
3. Ephesus
4. Columbia
5. 1978
6. Partially decomposed matter
7. Siddhartha
8. A group of Expressionist painters
9. East of Borneo
10. Skating

## FOREIGN WORDS AND PHRASES page 72

1. In private, or in secret
2. The majority, the masses
3. Tact
4. Please sit down
5. I'll be seeing you
6. An indispensable condition or qualification
7. Why?
8. Something done and no longer worth worrying about
9. Wet paint
10. How do you do?

## A MIXED BAG page 74
1. The CN Tower in Toronto
2. Lignite
3. A watch chain
4. Liquid tapped from maple trees
5. Charles Kingsley
6. At least 1000 years ago
7. Antique irridescent glass
8. The Great Wall of China
9. An Irish engagement ring
10. 19.3.

## THE WILD, WILD WEST page 76
1. Judge Roy Bean
2. A large covered wagon
3. They all died defending the Alamo
4. For eighteen months
5. Mississippi riverboats
6. Black Kettle – he was a Cheyenne chief
7. 1876
8. An unbranded calf
9. The Daltons
10. The stock of riding horses from which cowboys selected their mounts

## A MIXED BAG page 78
1. Gibraltar
2. An apparition of a living person
3. The cello
4. 1720
5. Forth
6. Europe
7. 1966
8. The seashore between high and low tides
9. Thirty
10. A breed of dog

## ART AND ARTISTS page 80
1. Sandro Botticelli
2. Woodcarving
3. Horses
4. Henry Moore
5. Franz Hals
6. Michelangelo
7. John Sell Cotman
8. A Kit-cat
9. Gustave Doré
10. Imperceptible transitions of tone from light to dark

## A MIXED BAG page 82
1. Denmark
2. Mercury
3. Ham House
4. Ole Rømer
5. New Holland
6. Aberystwyth
7. Vienna
8. 1968
9. Nelson
10. Kitchen staff at the Savoy

## THE RULES OF THE GAME page 84
1. 30.5 metres (100 feet)
2. Four points
3. White
4. The popping crease
5. 9 metres (10 yards)
6. The first player to reach seven points with a two-point lead
7. Sixteen
8. White canvas bags
9. American football
10. Bantamweight, Featherweight, Lightweight, Light welterweight

## A MIXED BAG page 86
1. Lagos
2. International Amateur Athletic Federation
3. Shrove Tuesday
4. Produce white blood cells
5. Neil Armstrong
6. Thirteen
7. The Egyptian pound
8. A shuttlecock
9. Rome
10. Edinburgh

## —OLOGIES page 88
1. Joints
2. Mosses
3. Crustaceans
4. Human activities
5. Internal parts
6. Water
7. The past history of life
8. Fire and heat
9. Soils
10. Tides

## A MIXED BAG page 90
1. 1813
2. A joey
3. It has a texture like bread
4. An English economist and statesman
5. A dark nebula in the Milky Way
6. The Black Sea
7. A museum
8. Hyde Park
9. The Queen
10. A Benedictine monastery

## DOWN BY THE RIVER page 92
1. The Amazon
2. The Shannon
3. Sydney
4. The Neva
5. The Arno
6. Shanghai
7. Addis Ababa
8. St Louis
9. The Loire
10. The Colorado

## A MIXED BAG page 94
1. Lake Superior
2. A volcano
3. Strategic Arms Limitation Talks
4. March 1985
5. Engelbert Humperdinck
6. A diamond in the British Crown Jewels
7. AD 785
8. Seven
9. A lively dance
10. A breed of cat

## ROMAN BRITAIN page 96
1. Ridge Way
2. Fishbourne
3. AD 120–123
4. Near St Albans
5. Richborough
6. Dover
7. Rome was sacked by the Goths
8. Deal
9. AD 60
10. It was the furthest point up the Thames ships could sail on the tide

## A MIXED BAG page 98
1. Giuseppe Verdi
2. East Wales
3. No rules
4. 1215
5. A network of nerves
6. On the border between Italy and Switzerland
7. Non-standard use of grammar
8. Dar es Salaam
9. AD 400 to AD 1000
10. A small fancy sponge cake

**COME RAIN, COME SHINE**
page 100
1. Hawaii
2. The north
3. A discharge of static electricity around the tips of tall objects
4. 1970
5. April and December
6. A storm
7. The air
8. A dry, warm wind, blowing down a mountain
9. Cumulonimbus
10. Red, orange, yellow, green, blue, indigo, violet

**A MIXED BAG** page 102
1. The Crimean War
2. Canada and the USA
3. Curling
4. In the Northern Indian Ocean
5. Thor
6. One billion
7. 11 September 1988
8. African languages
9. Muhammad Ali
10. An autumn crocus

**OLYMPIC GAMES** page 104
1. 1948
2. Sonja Henie
3. Michael Gross
4. 1976
5. The 1500 Metres
6. Larissa Latynina
7. 1972
8. Decathlon
9. The Javelin
10. Dressage

**A MIXED BAG** page 106
1. Ulan Bator
2. Almost 11,000,000
3. A roof with each face having two slopes
4. A Boeing B-17
5. Horns grow on both sexes of some animals and continue to grow all their lives; antlers grow on male deer and are renewed
6. A suspended grating which can be raised or lowered at the entrance of a castle
7. Susie Orbach
8. A period of continuous play in polo
9. 1914
10. British Honduras

**NOVEL EXPERIENCE** page 109
1. *The Pickwick Papers*
2. George Smiley
3. *Pride and Prejudice*
4. Malcolm Bradbury
5. Reddleman
6. *Gorky Park*
7. *Diary of a Nobody*
8. Dick Francis
9. Empress of Blandings
10. Catherine Cookson

**A MIXED BAG** page 112
1. Roger Bannister
2. Repellent and unattractive
3. 1095
4. Bach
5. A specially endowed chapel
6. 1952
7. A rounded hollow in a mountainside
8. The French Resistance in the Second World War
9. They have all walked on the moon
10. Soil which turns to sticky mud in the rain

## THE RULING CLASS page 114
1. Edward, the Black Prince
2. All of the people mentioned
3. Bruton Street, London
4. No one
5. The Duchess of Gloucester
6. 1978
7. 20 January to 11 December 1936
8. Princess Michael of Kent
9. The Duke and Duchess of Kent
10. Prince Andrew

## A MIXED BAG page 116
1. Hastings, Sandwich, Dover, Romney, Rye
2. Anne Boleyn
3. St Margaret's Bay
4. Plaice
5. Seventy-four
6. Godmersham
7. William Harvey
8. 1963
9. Broadstairs
10. Waltham Abbey

## SCIENTISTS AND INVENTORS page 118
1. Charles Babbage
2. Benjamin Franklin
3. Explanation of the photoelectric effect which is the basis of the atom
4. Georg and Laszlo Biro
5. The refrigerator
6. Antoine Becquerel
7. Nicolaus Copernicus
8. Dynamite
9. The Galapagos
10. Gregor Mendel

## A MIXED BAG page 121
1. Johnny Weissmuller
2. A team of display helicopters
3. Minster Son
4. Weight
5. Vasco da Gama
6. 10.1°C
7. 15–16 October 1987
8. The RAF's
9. Russia
10. Ian Woosnam

## CARS OVER THE YEARS page 123
1. 1959
2. Morris and Austin
3. Alvis
4. *Bullitt*
5. Forty-four years
6. The top car is 1980s, below it is 1930s, 1950s and 1960s (bottom car)
7. Ferrari
8. They were all three-wheelers
9. A cabriolet
10. Jaguar

## A MIXED BAG page 126
1. Music intended to be played in a small room, with few performers
2. 54.8 million
3. A fish
4. 9640 kilometres
5. They were all royal houses of England
6. In 1485
7. 23° N
8. Smoky yellow or brown
9. World Health Organisation
10. 1967

## ON THE BOX page 128

1. Joan Hickson
2. BBC 2
3. Jack and Vera Duckworth in *Coronation Street*
4. *Gardeners' World*
5. They are both set in Australia
6. An antiques dealer
7. Cagney and Lacey
8. *M.A.S.H.*
9. Mike Morris and Kathy Taylor
10. Chris Serle and Paul Heiney

## A MIXED BAG page 130

1. 1972
2. Fifth
3. The February Revolution
4. Balmoral Castle
5. Mount Rushmore
6. Plaited leaves
7. Secrete insulin
8. Black
9. Two horizontal bars above and below the midpoint of the vertical bar, the lower longer than the upper
10. A customs and economics union of the above countries

## MAKING DATES page 132

1. The fourth century BC
2. 1969
3. 1815
4. 1040
5. 1899
6. 1415
7. 1901
8. 1381
9. 1963
10. 1170

## A MIXED BAG page 134

1. The Chancellor of the Exchequer
2. India
3. One in 5,000,000
4. D'Artagnan
5. France
6. Radio 4
7. 10 am
8. Peking
9. In 1977
10. To hurry slowly

## THE WORKS OF THE BARD page 136

1. Miranda
2. Mark Antony
3. *Twelfth Night*
4. Bassanio
5. Romeo and Juliet
6. *Henry V*
7. Valentine and Proteus
8. Macduff
9. Desdemona's
10. Richard III

## A MIXED BAG page 138

1. Antarctica
2. Away from the Sun
3. Radiation activity
4. T.S. Eliot
5. The second Saturday in June
6. Alabama
7. 1907
8. 7.30 pm
9. The ampère
10. 1642

## FUNNY HA HA page 140

1. Peter Sellers
2. Ken Dodd
3. Peter Cook
4. Alastair Sim
5. Joan Rivers
6. Anthony Aloysius Hancock
7. Hercules
8. Mel Brooks
9. *Monty Python's Flying Circus*
10. Margaret Dumont

**A MIXED BAG** page 143
1. A naturally absorbent clay
2. Nearly one in seven
3. 'O Canada'
4. A kit
5. The Duke of York's
6. Fermented palm tree sap
7. The USA
8. A method of drying and preserving flowers
9. Telstar 2
10. A legal notice

**RECORD BREAKERS** page 145
1. A giant sequoia tree
2. 120 years 8 months
3. The Sears Tower, Chicago
4. 3500
5. Blackpool
6. 8 ft 11 in
7. 250 metres (273 yards)
8. Richmond Castle, Yorkshire
9. Glasgow
10. 44.9 mph (71 kph)

**A MIXED BAG** page 147
1. 2000 BC to 1200 BC
2. An easy catch
3. Billy Bunter
4. Hamilton
5. 1947
6. Belgium
6. A carpenter's tool
8. The Lord Chancellor
9. Four
10. Abyssinia

**CRIME AND CRIMINALS** page 149
1. Five
2. 1955
3. The brains behind the Great Train Robbery
4. Scarface
5. John Christie
6. Sell the Eiffel Tower
7. The victim in the Red Barn murder in 1827
8. Reginald and Ronald
9. Robert Franklin Stroud
10. Bonnie and Clyde

**A MIXED BAG** page 151
1. James VI
2. 1945
3. The Greek word for 'fish' was composed of the initial letters of the words meaning 'Jesus Christ, Son of God, Saviour'
4. Diogenes
5. Palladium
6. Frequency
7. Turquoise
8. A tributary stream flowing into a larger stream or river
9. 1564
10. A4

**MUSICAL MISCELLANY** page 153
1. Tchaikovsky
2. The 1950s
3. Bertolt Brecht
4. *Pizzicato*
5. *Tosca*
6. Four
7. A Venetian boating song
8. Benjamin Britten
9. The piano
10. 'So do all women'

**A MIXED BAG** page 155
1. A sow
2. 2400 km
3. A resin
4. Fifty-six
5. A Scottish liquid measurement
6. A republic
7. In Porthcurno
8. Sir Humphry Davy
9. Chelmsford
10. St Ives

## FUNNY PECULIAR page 157

1. The passengers had to jettison their clothes and so arrived naked
2. Jayne Mansfield
3. A bear
4. 150,000,000
5. Venus
6. Twenty-six
7. A toy
8. 40 mph/64 kmh
9. Clark Gable
10. King James I

## A MIXED BAG page 159

1. Everton
2. A river mouth
3. A ballet dancer
4. The leg
5. 54
6. 6 December
7. January 1986
8. The EEPTU
9. Sweden
10. Jane

## CREEPY CRAWLIES page 161

1. A beetle
2. Four to five years
3. Aphids
4. Butterflies
5. 5.5 inches (140 millimetres)
6. Nectar
7. The dragonfly
8. The springtail
9. 130 times
10. The stag beetle

## A MIXED BAG page 163

1. 500 metres
2. An island
3. Kestrel
4. Thirteen
5. Francis II
6. A Canadian island in the St Lawrence River
7. 1927
8. By that very fact
9. 53%
10. Boris Becker

## POETRY CORNER page 165

1. Percy Bysshe Shelley
2. Playing tennis
3. A wedding guest
4. Rupert Brooke
5. 'He Wishes for the Cloths of Heaven'
6. John Keats
7. Sicily
8. *A Midsummer Night's Dream*
9. Lord Byron
10. Floating, dead, in a boat down the river

## A MIXED BAG page 168

1. Light blue and yellow
2. Princess Alexandra and the Hon. Angus Ogilvy
3. Chocolates
4. Squash
5. Bonn
6. A Russian alcoholic drink
7. The staircase
8. Baseball
9. Portsmouth
10. Russian

## THE BODY BEAUTIFUL page 170

1. The neck
2. Four
3. A small bone in the leg
4. 3 pounds/1530 grams
5. The chief artery of the body
6. Triceps
7. In the hip
8. Concerned with the kidneys
9. A membrane lining the abdominal cavity
10. The pituitary

## A MIXED BAG page 172
1. Cragside House, Rothbury, Morpeth
2. A person who pulls ale
3. 1889
4. The widowed and their children
5. Innumerable
6. P.T. Barnum
7. Three
8. Woolsthorpe Manor, Colsterworth
9. A grape
10. The USA

## AS THEY SAY IN THE USA
page 174
1. An aubergine
2. A municipal school
3. Slipper of bacon
4. A courgette
5. A tenon saw
6. A maisonette
7. Paraffin
8. A draught excluder
8. Your signature
10. An underground walkway

## A MIXED BAG page 176
1. Alexandra
2. Yellow
3. May
4. 1965
5. Galileo Galilei
6. Florida
7. Lead
8. Deep blue
9. Greenland
10. Kingston-upon-Thames

## GETTING THERE page 178
1. Euston
2. The A38
3. Stranraer to Larne
4. The Bakerloo Line
5. York
6. Manchester
7. Newcastle
8. Evesham
9. The Test
10. Clacton-on-Sea, Harwich, Aldeburgh, Lowestoft

## A MIXED BAG page 181
1. The central portion of the Earth
2. 1727
3. US dollars in a European holding for short-term finance
4. Africa
5. Ed Mirvish
6. Rudolf Diesel
7. Difficult or laboured breathing
8. A plant
9. A fungal infection
10. Basingstoke

## ADJECTIVAL ANALYSIS
page 183
1. Idealistic
2. Weakening
3. Insincere
4. Everlasting
5. Bewildered
6. Boastful
7. Scanty
8. Undeveloped
9. Pastoral
10. Childish

## A MIXED BAG page 185
1. The Duke of Windsor
2. 19
3. A snapdragon
4. Form a guard of honour at the Vatican
5. Damascus
6. Denominazione d'origine controllata
7. Breeds of cattle
8. 'While Shepherds Watched Their Flocks By Night'
9. Grace Kelly
10. Hampshire

## FEATHERED FRIENDS page 187

1. The barn owl
2. The goldcrest
3. A bird of prey which eats birds and small mammals
4. The avocet
5. The woodpecker
6. The sparrow
7. The ostrich
8. 106 mph/170 kph
9. Ducks
10. Swans

## A MIXED BAG page 189

1. The Dauphin
2. A town
3. Syria
4. A small group of intriguers
5. 1864
6. A spittoon
7. The USA
8. 1962
9. 68 kilos
10. New York

## WHO SAID IT? page 191

1. Dr Johnson
2. Oscar Wilde
3. Jerome K. Jerome
4. Henry Ford
5. Dorothy Parker
6. George Bernard Shaw
7. Mae West
8. King Henri IV of France
9. Oscar Wilde
10. Henry Fielding

## A MIXED BAG page 194

1. Queen's Park Rangers
2. West Germany
3. The Indian Ocean
4. The *Gipsy Moth*
5. *David Copperfield*
6. Vinegar
7. A heavy horse
8. Jane Seymour
9. Berlin
10. Wear crowns of lighted candles

## FEARSOME PHOBIAS page 196

1. Cats
2. Solitude
3. Thunder
4. Speaking aloud
5. Snakes
6. Open spaces
7. God
8. Dampness
9. Foreigners
10. Animals

## A MIXED BAG page 198

1. Kent
2. 1968
3. To scrape the body after bathing
4. Reading
5. Seven
6. Duke of Cambridge
7. Liverpool
8. A picture posed by people
9. Mineral
10. At Runnymede

## OCEAN WAVES page 200

1. The South China Sea
2. The South Atlantic
3. The Tasman Sea
4. 139,670,000 square miles/ 361,740,000 square kilometres
5. The Arabian Sea
6. The Caspian Sea
7. In the Antarctic
8. Corsica and Sardinia
9. Between Iceland and Greenland
10. Pacific

## A MIXED BAG page 202

1. 98%
2. 1965
3. A semi-precious stone
4. A lime tree
5. 1901–9
6. In Poland
7. In 1337
8. Blue
9. 29 September
10. W1

## CEREMONIES AND CUSTOMS
page 204
1. 1000 years
2. The Gurning Contest
3. 'Decapitate' him
4. Unknown
5. Pieces of cloth
6. Every seven years
7. When the tides are too high
8. The 'luck' is broken
9. The death of protestant martyrs
10. Burrs

## A MIXED BAG page 206
1. President Zia
2. Sue Townsend
3. A ship loaded with toxic waste
4. 51,000,000
5. April 1986
6. The first dog allowed into the House of Commons
7. 1666
8. A butterfly
9. 340
10. The nasturtium

## AROUND BRITAIN page 208
1. London and Leeds
2. On the Lincolnshire coast
3. East
4. Ullapool
5. Saltash
6. Cape Wrath
7. The Romney, Hythe and Dymchurch Railway
8. Near Northampton
9. Gloucestershire
10. Off the North Wales coast

## A MIXED BAG page 210
1. 60 grams
2. The Famous Five characters created by Enid Blyton
3. Near John O'Groats
4. Enzo Ferrari
5. A potter
6. Sri Lanka
7. The Princess Royal
8. Parts of Lincolnshire
9. The Al-Fayed brothers
10. Newmarket

## ABBREVIATIONS page 212
1. Advisory, Conciliation and Arbitration Service
2. Royal Horticultural Society
3. Quasi-non-governmental organisation
4. Licentiate of the Royal Academy of Music
5. National Aeronautics and Space Administration
6. *Ad libitum* – at pleasure
7. Member of the Institute of Mechanical Engineers
8. Radio detection and ranging
9. Deoxyribonucleic acid
10 Associate of the Royal Institute of Chartered Surveyors

## A MIXED BAG page 214
1. Television comedians
2. They all must be notified to a medical officer for environmental health
3. 36.8°C
4. Pink
5. Billie Jean King
6. Standardised Northern Chinese
7. The *News of the World*
8. A film director
9. Dostoyevsky
10. Lung cancer

## RADIO TIME page 216
1. Jenni Murray
2. 7.30 am
3. Comedy
4. Radio 3
5. Brian and Jennifer Aldridge
6. Nigel Forde
7. The arts
8. Sue Lawley
9. Round the clock
10. Robert Robinson

## A MIXED BAG page 218
1. In the northern and southern hemispheres
2. Stoneware
3. Caribou
4. Robert Service
5. 177,000 sq km
6. Loud
7. 1829
8. The Queen, the Dyers Company and the Vintners Company
9. Stamps
10. The Thames' Boatmen's Race

## THE PLAY'S THE THING
page 220
1. *Pygmalion*
2. Anton Chekhov
3. *The Importance of Being Earnest*
4. John Gay
5. Tennessee Williams
6. Molière
7. A butler
8. Ben Jonson
9. William Congreve
10. *Kiss Me, Kate*